HOME MATHEMATICS

A B Tookey *Dip Ed*

Head of Newsom Department, Thomas Peacocke School, Rye
Formerly Head of Mathematics Department, Rye County Secondary School

New metric edition

Longman

LONGMAN GROUP LTD
London
Associated companies, branches and representatives throughout the world

First edition © A B Tookey 1967
New metric edition © Longman Group Ltd 1971
All rights reserved. No part of this publication may be reproduced,
stored in a retrieval system or transmitted in any form or by any
means, electronic, mechanical, photocopying, recording or otherwise,
without the prior permission of the copyright owner.

First published 1967
New metric edition first published 1971
Third impression 1972
ISBN 0 582 20810 6

Made and printed in Great Britain by
William Clowes & Sons, Limited, London, Beccles and Colchester

Also in this series:
Starting Statistics by K Lewis and W Ward

Preface to new metric edition

This edition uses the new British decimal currency system almost throughout the text. There are only occasional references to 'pounds, shillings and pence' and these occur where the various authorities have not yet decided upon values and costs in the new system.

Full information about decimal currency can be obtained from the Decimal Currency Board, Standard House, 27 Northumberland Avenue, London, WC2. Little mention has been made, however, of the old 'sixpence' whose future is relatively uncertain. South Africa was in a similar position over their 3d piece which they replaced by a $2\frac{1}{2}$ cent coin. This, in fact, proved to be unpopular and has since been withdrawn.

All measurements of length and capacity etc. are shown in the metric system i.e. metres, litres, with some practice in conversion.

A. B. TOOKEY

1970

Preface to the first edition

Many CSE boards are now offering a syllabus as part of their examination in mathematics, which is devoted to the mathematical aspects of everyday life. Numerous textbooks offer explanations and examples on these topics as an incidental part of their contents, but very few are devoted entirely to those mathematical situations which we all encounter as soon as we start work and set up a home.

This book, the first in a new series *Mathematics at Work*, has been specifically written to meet the needs of pupils and teachers alike by bringing together, in one volume, as many of these topics of 'home mathematics' as possible.

As well as being directed at the pupil studying for CSE mathematics, it is hoped that all fourth- and fifth-year non-examination or 'Newsom' pupils will find this book of help.

I would like to record my personal thanks to the Midland Bank Limited for many helpful suggestions and for permission to reproduce their cheques and paying-in slip, to the Hastings and Thanet Building Society for much useful information and for permission to use their table of mortgage repayments, and to the Postmaster-General for permission to quote facts and information from the *Post Office Guide*.

My thanks are also due to the following professional and business friends for their help in reading, criticizing or correcting particular sections of the book: Mrs M. Woolard, Mr B. J. E. Swanton, Mr J. K. Wainwright, and Mr R. W. W. Webb.

Finally, I should like to thank my wife for typing, checking and correcting this book and without whose help this book would never have been published.

A. B. TOOKEY

1967

Contents

1 Wages and salaries

Most people go to work at some time in their lives and are paid for doing so. Payment is made in many different ways. The most common methods of calculating wages are described below:

Payment by the hour

Many people engaged in practical and production work—for example, building trades, some engineering trades, lorry drivers and others connected with transport—are paid for each hour that they work at a particular rate. This rate is generally the result of negotiation between the trade unions and employers.

Payment by results or piecework

This method of payment is based upon the number of articles produced by an employee or group of employees in a given time. For example, a man might be machining certain engine parts or fitting other parts together in an engine and payment is made according to the number of parts made or assembled in a week. The time that the operation should take is determined by consultation, so that a man can earn a reasonable wage if he works at the agreed rate. This method penalizes the lazy, inefficient, slow or late worker and rewards the skilful and quick.

Commission

This is a varying sum paid to salesmen and people in similar occupations. It is usually a fraction of the cost of the goods they have sold. Some people, but not all, are paid a weekly or annual wage in addition to the commission and they are usually entitled to certain expenses for travelling, postage, stationery and entertaining clients to whom they wish to sell goods.

Salary

Many people are paid a certain amount of money for a year's work; for example, teachers, civil servants and bank clerks. This amount increases for some years by definite amounts, these increases are called 'increments'. Representatives of employers and employees usually discuss these different salaries, called a 'salary scale', before any changes are made.

Payment by the hour

Example

Jack Brown works for 44 hours at $22\frac{1}{2}$p an hour. Find his total (gross) pay.

Solution

$44 \times 22\frac{1}{2}$p $= £9{\cdot}90$.

Exercises 1A

1. Copy the table shown below and calculate the gross (or total) pay due to each man.

Name	Trade	Rate per hour	Time	Gross pay
Andrews, C.	Joiner	22p	41 hours	
Jones, W.	Painter	23p	26 hours	
Thomas, R.	Bricklayer	$19\frac{1}{2}$p	33 hours	

It is customary for people calculating gross pay, as in the example above, to use a *ready reckoner*.

2. Complete the ready reckoner shown below

No. of hours	$\frac{1}{2}$	1	2	3	4	5	6	7	8	9	10	50
Amount		22p	44p	66p								

3. Use the completed table to find the amount for
   a. 17 hours;   b. 25 hours;   c. $38\frac{1}{2}$ hours.

4. The number of hours worked in a week varies with a person's occupation, but the majority work a basic week of between 40 and 45 hours. Construct a ready reckoner in the form shown below for all the hours 40 to 45 including $\frac{1}{2}$ hours and for all the rates of pay from 19p to 25p and one for half a new penny.

	$\frac{1}{2}$p	19p	20p	21p	22p	23p	24p	25p
		£	£	£	£	£	£	£
40	20	7·60	8·00	8·40	8·80	9·20	9·60	10·00
$40\frac{1}{2}$	$20\frac{1}{4}$							
41	$20\frac{1}{2}$							
$41\frac{1}{2}$	21							
42	21							
$42\frac{1}{2}$	$21\frac{1}{2}$							
43	$21\frac{1}{2}$							
$43\frac{1}{2}$								
44								
$44\frac{1}{2}$								
45								

5. Use the ready reckoner you have made to calculate the wages in the following cases:

   a. 40 hours at 24p per hour
   b. 44 hours at 23p per hour
   c. $43\frac{1}{2}$ hours at 22p per hour
   d. 41 hours at $22\frac{1}{2}$p per hour
   e. $44\frac{1}{2}$ hours at $24\frac{1}{2}$p per hour
   f. $42\frac{1}{2}$ hours at $23\frac{1}{2}$p per hour.

Overtime

People who are paid by the hour are often paid extra money if they work more than a certain number of hours in a week. These extra hours are called 'overtime'.

Overtime is usually paid at one of the following rates:

   a. Basic rate *plus* one-quarter of the basic rate—this is called 'time and a quarter'.

   b. Basic rate *plus* one-half of the basic rate—this is called 'time and a half'.

   c. Twice the basic rate—this is called 'double time'.

Exercises 1B

What is the overtime rate at (*a*) time and a quarter

(*b*) time and a half, for the following basic rates?

(*i*) 16p; (*ii*) 22p; (*iii*) 17p; (*iv*) 23p.

If a man works indoors, e.g. in a factory, and is paid by this method, he will probably record his hours of attendance on a card which he places in a time-recording clock, or 'clocking-on machine' as it is often called. When the card is placed in the slot provided, the machine records the same time on the card as is shown on the clock on the machine.

The employee gets his card stamped four times each day

   i. when he arrives at work in the morning,

  ii. when he stops work for his midday meal,

 iii. when he starts work again after his midday meal,

 iv. when he stops work in the evening.

The times on the card could look like this:

	ON	OFF	ON	OFF
Monday	07.28	12.02	12.57	5.02

What time do you think work was due to start each morning and afternoon? How long was a full working day?

Some firms only require their employees to 'clock on' and do not permit their staff to leave the premises during working hours. These hours are recorded on a time sheet by the wages clerk, who then calculates the weekly wage.

Lorry drivers and farm workers carry their time sheets about with them. They often start and finish at odd times and in unusual places. For instance, a farm worker could be employed at some considerable distance from the main farm buildings and a lorry driver could be on a journey which keeps him away all night. Consequently each man would record on his time sheet or log book the time when he started and finished work and any periods during which he did not work; for example, lunch time. Two days' entries on a farm worker's weekly time sheet could look like this:

Name J. Little   *Week ending* 26th March

Day of week	Where working. State farm and field	Time started	Description of work done	Time finished	Total unpaid breaks	Hours worked Ord.	Over-time
Mon a.m.	Brown Edge Farm	06.30	Cleaning ditch	12.00	15 min	5	$\frac{1}{4}$
p.m.	7-acre field	13.00	Cleaning ditch	18.00	—	4	1
Tues a.m.	Brown Edge Farm	06.30	Hedging	12.15	15 min	5	$\frac{1}{2}$
p.m.	Jack's Meadow	13.00	Hedging	19.00	30 min	4	$1\frac{1}{2}$

How long is J. Little's ordinary working day? Would this be the same all the year round?

Exercises 1C

1. From the time card illustrated below:

Calculate

   a. the number of hours worked by Jackson in the week

   b. the number of hours he works at each rate and his total pay if his rates of pay are:

      i. a 42-hour week at 32p per hour,

      ii. week-day overtime at time and a quarter,

      iii. Saturday work at time and a half,

      iv. double time for Sundays.

Why are 07.41 and 16.31 underlined?

Note. Employees would be expected to clock on before or at 07.30 and 13.00 and clock off at or after 12.00 and 17.00. Late arrival or early departure is calculated in quarter-hours. Hence clocking on at 07.31 or clocking off at 16.58 would lose the employee a quarter of an hour in each case.

Works No. 637
Name   JACKSON, John   *Week ending* 21st September

PRECISION PRODUCTS

	IN	OUT	IN	OUT	IN	OUT	TOTAL
M	07.29	12.00	13.00	17.01			
Tu	07.26	12.02	12.57	<u>16.31</u>			
W	<u>07.41</u>	12.00	12.58	17.02			
Th	07.30	12.01	12.59	17.03	17.29	20.01	
F	07.30	12.03	12.57	17.01	17.28	20.00	
S	08.00	12.00	13.00	16.00			
Sun			13.00	17.02			

	Hours	Rate	£
Ordinary Time			
Overtime *(i)* (Rate $\times$ $1\frac{1}{4}$)			
(ii) (Rate $\times$ $1\frac{1}{2}$)			
(iii) (Rate $\times$ 2)			
Total			

2. A driver works 56 hours in one week. His basic rate is 24p per hour.

  a. What is the rate per hour of overtime at 'time and a quarter'?

  b. If he is paid at the basic rate for the first 42 hours in each week (this is called 'a 42-hour week') how many hours of overtime does he work?

  c. What is he paid for his overtime?

  d. What are his total earnings for the week?

  3. On a certain building site, men are paid at different rates depending on their trade.
  The table shows a time sheet for some of the men employed on the site. They all work a 44-hour week. Ordinary overtime (Monday to Friday) is paid at time and a quarter and Saturday working is paid at time and a half *only* if 44 hours have already been completed.

Note. Many calculations involve fractions of a penny. Therefore, always calculate as exactly as possible and give your final answer in a sensible form, in this case to the nearest half a new penny.

	Basic Rate per hour	Mon	Tue	Wed	Thur	Fri	Sat
	new pence						
Allenbury	21	6	8	8	7	9	4
Black	18	$8\frac{1}{2}$	$8\frac{1}{2}$	10	$8\frac{1}{2}$	10	4
Crosby	22	6	8	7	6	6	2
Ewart	28	8	8	8	8	8	4
Foster	23	$7\frac{1}{2}$	11	$7\frac{1}{2}$	9	9	$3\frac{1}{2}$
Godden	$19\frac{1}{2}$	5	8	10	8	6	—
Hunt	$24\frac{1}{2}$	9	9	10	$9\frac{1}{2}$	$9\frac{1}{2}$	—

  a. Find the total hours worked by each man.

  b. How many hours overtime did each man work?

  c. What are the two rates of overtime pay for each man?

  d. How much is each man paid for overtime?

  e. Find the total earnings for each man.

  4. The table opposite shows the time worked by four men employed by an electrical firm.

	Mon	*Tue*	*Wed*	*Thur*	*Fri*	*Sat*
Allen	07.30–12.30	07.30–12.30	07.30–12.30	08.15–12.30	08.00–12.30	07.00–12.00
	13.30–17.00	13.30–17.00	13.30–18.30	13.30–17.45	13.30–18.00	
Brown	07.30–12.30	08.00–12.00	10.00–12.30	07.30–12.30	07.30–12.00	07.30–13.00
	14.00–18.30	13.00–19.00	13.30–16.30	13.30–20.30	13.00–21.00	
Cook	09.00–12.30	09.00–12.00	09.00–12.00	09.00–12.00	09.00–12.00	
	13.30–18.00	13.00–18.00	13.00–19.00	13.00–17.30		
Dodds	07.00–13.00	07.00–13.00	07.00–12.00	07.00–13.00	07.00–12.00	07.00–13.00
	14.00–18.00	14.00–18.00	13.30–16.30	14.15–18.15	13.00–20.00	

Copy the chart below and fill in the blanks so as to show the number of hours worked per day (Allen has been worked for you).

	Mon	*Tue*	*Wed*	*Thur*	*Fri*	*Total*	*Sat*	*Total*
Allen	$8\frac{1}{2}$	$8\frac{1}{2}$	10	$8\frac{1}{2}$	9	$44\frac{1}{2}$	5	$49\frac{1}{2}$
Brown								
Cook								
Dodds								

Mr Allen's rate of pay is 24p per hour for a 42-hour week.
Mr Brown's rate of pay is 21p per hour for a 41-hour week.
Mr Cook's rate of pay is 17p per hour for a 44-hour week.
Mr Dodd's rate of pay is $24\frac{1}{2}$p per hour for a 43-hour week.

For all the men overtime on Monday to Friday is at 'time and a quarter' and on Saturday 'time and a half' as long as the requisite number of hours per week have been completed.

Copy and complete the wage-check forms (Allen has been worked for you):

Allen 42 hours at 24p $= 42 \times 24p = £10·08$
$2\frac{1}{2}$ hours at 24p $\times 1\frac{1}{4} = 2\frac{1}{2} \times 30p = £ 0·75$
5 hours at 24p $\times 1\frac{1}{2} = 5 \times 36p = £ 1·80$

Total wage $= £12·63$

Repeat for Brown, Cook and Dodds.

Piecework

This system is used in many manufacturing industries where employees are paid in proportion to the number of articles made. Bonuses are often paid as an additional incentive to encourage greater production and to reduce waste of time and material.

Example

A man is paid $\frac{1}{2}$p for each part of an electric fire that he sprays up to 400 in each day. After that he receives 1p each. He sprays 420 on Monday, 480 on Tuesday, 416 on Wednesday and 320 on Thursday.

    a. If he sprays 500 on Friday what are his week's earnings?

    b. If he wishes to earn £14 how many must he spray on Friday?

Solution

  a. Monday   400 at $\frac{1}{2}$p +   20 at 1p = £2·00 + £0·20 = £ 2·20
        Tuesday   400 at $\frac{1}{2}$p +   80 at 1p = £2·00 + £0·80 = £ 2·80
        Wednesday 400 at $\frac{1}{2}$p +   16 at 1p = £2·00 + £0·16 = £ 2.16
        Thursday   320 at $\frac{1}{2}$p +   = £1·60 +   = £ 1·60
        Friday   400 at $\frac{1}{2}$p + 100 at 1p = £2·00 + £1·00 = £ 3·00

                                                        Total = £11·76

  b. Monday–Thursday as (*a*) = £8·76
      On Friday he must earn   £5·24
      400 at $\frac{1}{2}$p = £2·00; this leaves £3·24 still to be earned
      £3·24 = 324p
∴ he must spray 724 parts.

Exercises 1D

1. A small engineering component is machined and undergoes the following operations:

Name	Operation	Rate	Number produced per day
Hughes	Turning	2p each	190
Roberts	Milling	$17\frac{1}{2}$p per 10*	200
Thomson	Drilling	6p per 10	500
Williams	Grinding	14p per 10	260

Find the amount earned by each man in a day.

* Equivalent to $1\frac{3}{4}$p each. It is likely that industry will continue to use fractions of a penny (new penny) although they will always round totals off to the nearest new half-penny.

2. A girl is paid 20p for machining ten teddy bears. How many must she complete in a week in order to earn the basic minimum wage of £4·56 for a 5-day 38-hour week?

How much time is allowed to machine each teddy bear?

If her bonus rate is 25p per ten (i.e. when her earnings exceed £4·56 a week), how many will she have made if her earnings are £6·76?

3. In which of the following three jobs is the total weekly payment greatest? By how much does it exceed the other two?

a. $52\frac{1}{2}$ hours (no overtime) at 31p per hour.

b. 44 hours at 30p and $8\frac{1}{2}$ hours overtime at 'time and a quarter'.

c. Drilling 80 brass plates per hour at 41p per 100 for a 48-hour week.

4. Betty Jones is paid 4p for assembling a part of a record player. She is paid a weekly bonus of an extra 2p for each one she assembles over 250 a week. If the factory produces more than 4000 a week, each employee receives an additional bonus of $1\frac{1}{2}$p per record player.

	Betty Jones	Total factory output per day
Day	Number assembled	
Monday	51	250
Tuesday	48	750
Wednesday	54	850
Thursday	53	1100
Friday	56	1145

a. Find:

i. Betty Jones's basic weekly pay without bonuses at 4p per part assembled,

ii. her own assembly bonus,

iii. the total number of record players produced in this week,

iv. the total production bonus per person,

v. her gross earnings for the week.

b. If in another week she assembled 308 parts and the factory produced a steady average of 832 parts per day, calculate

i. the additional bonus that each employee received that week,

ii. Betty Jones's earnings for that week.

Commission

Commercial travellers, agents and some shop assistants are often paid an amount of money in addition to their weekly wage or annual salary, calculated on the amount or value of goods they sell. This additional payment is called 'commission'.

Example

A traveller receives $1\frac{1}{2}$ per cent commission on all his sales

   a. Find what he would receive in a week when he sold goods to the value of £1000.

   b. What is the value of the goods he has sold if the commission he receives is £12?

Solution

$$a.\ \ \frac{1\frac{1}{2}}{100} \times 1000 = \frac{3}{200} \times \overset{5}{\cancel{1000}} = £15.$$

$\therefore$ His commission in that week would be £15.

$$b.\ \ \frac{1\frac{1}{2}}{100} \times £x = £12$$

$$x = \frac{1200}{1\frac{1}{2}} = \frac{2400}{3} = £800.$$

$\therefore$ He sells £800 worth of goods.

Exercises 1E

   1. A commercial traveller is paid £10 per week and commission on all weekly sales over £200 of $2\frac{1}{2}$p in the £.

   Find his total weekly earnings (wage + commission), in the following weeks.

Week 1	Week 2	Week 3	Week 4
Sales £250	Sales £480	Sales £180	Sales £300

   2. A shop assistant selling electrical goods is paid $2\frac{1}{2}$ per cent on all sales up to £200 per week and 4 per cent thereafter.

   a. Find his commission in the weeks when his sales were
      i. £160; *ii.* £350; *iii.* £265.

   b. What are his sales if his commission is: *i.* £6; *ii.* £14·40.

   3. A departmental store pays different commissions in different departments. Find the total weekly wage in each of the following cases:

Department	Basic wage	Commission	Total sales
	£		£
Haberdashery	7·25	8p in the £	54
Carpets	10·25	1 per cent	320
Linens	8·00	$2\frac{1}{2}$p in the £	84
Bedding	8·50	$2\frac{1}{2}$ per cent	100

4. A man is paid $4\frac{1}{2}$ per cent of the value of all goods sold. Find the value of the goods he sells in a year in order to earn £1 350.

5. A senior traveller is paid $1\frac{1}{2}$ per cent of the value of goods sold for the first £50000, 1 per cent of the value of the next £50000, $\frac{1}{2}$ per cent of the value of the next £50000 and $\frac{1}{4}$ per cent of all goods sold after that in each year. In addition he receives a basic salary of £15 per week, a car allowance of £500 per year and a general expenses allowance of £10 per week.

Calculate his total annual income, including allowances, in the four years when his sales were as follows:

1966	£80000
1967	£120000
1968	£160000
1969	£205000

Salary

People who are paid a salary, e.g. teachers, secretaries and Government employees, are paid a definite amount for a year's work. Very rarely are overtime or bonuses paid. The annual salary is divided into twelve equal parts which is usually paid about the end of the month.

Exercises 1F

1. What is the monthly payment for each of the following salaries?
a. £480; *b.* £645; *c.* £738; *d.* £1028·70.

2. A secretary's salary is £480 per annum on her appointment, with five annual increments of £20 and four of £30, and a final increment after 10 years of £40. (Give your answers to the nearest new penny.)

a. her annual salary after 4 and 6 years' service,

b. her monthly salary during her fourth, eighth and tenth years,

c. by how much her monthly salary changes between the minimum and maximum salaries on the scale.

3. A man is offered the choice of the following salary scales:

A Starting salary £700 and an increase of 10 per cent per annum of the salary received the previous year, for seven years (all amounts calculated to the nearest whole £).

OR

B Starting salary £700 and three increments of £80 per annum followed by four increments of £85 per annum.

    a. Calculate all the salaries on each scale.

    b. In which year are the salaries the same?

    c. Draw graphs of each salary scale for the first 15 years.

    d. Draw graphs of the cumulative total amount received on each scale for 10 years.

    e. How long does it take for a man on scale A to earn as much altogether as a man on scale B (use the graph)?

    f. In which year does each scale give a salary in excess of £20 per week?

Exercises 1G

    1. What do you understand by the terms:

    a. Gross income

    b. Net income

    c. Time and a half

    d. Overtime

    e. A 44-hour week

    f. Piecework

    g. Commission

    h. Salary

    j. Annual increment?

Find references to some of these terms in the newspaper, cut them out and use them to illustrate your answer.

    2. Give three examples of each of the types of payment described in this chapter. Try to find different occupations from those which have been mentioned in this chapter.

    3. Ask an employee of your local Department of Employment and Productivity and your Youth Employment Office to obtain some accurate rates of pay for some local occupations.

    4. Inquire in your locality about:

    a. different types of payment—obtain some definite information,

    b. rates of pay per hour and payments by results (piecework), *c.* commission on sales—try a large store, an important garage which sells cars and any travelling or door-to-door salesman,

d. those people whose jobs are salaried—find out about salary scales— what is the Whitley Council salary scale?—how often are salary scales revised?

2 Deductions from income and methods of payment

Before an employee receives his wages or salary, his employer makes certain deductions. These are: *a*. Income Tax (PAYE); *b*. National Insurance Contributions; *c*. Superannuation or Trade Union Contributions.

The amount left after deductions have been made is called the *net income*.

Income tax

As this is deducted from your pay as you earn it and before you receive it and is paid directly to the Government by your employer, it is called Pay as You Earn—PAYE.

To calculate the exact amount of tax each individual should pay is a complicated matter, but certain fundamental ideas are fairly straightforward and these will be discussed below.

Before calculating the amount to be paid in tax, certain allowances are made against the gross income.

These allowances are not taxed and are occasionally changed by the Chancellor of the Exchequer in his budgets.

Earned income allowance
This is $\frac{2}{9}$ (two-ninths) of the first £4005 and $\frac{1}{9}$ (one-ninth) of the next £5940 of *net* pay after deducting travelling expenses, superannuation contributions and certain other expenses.

The personal allowance is £465 for a married man and £325 in all other cases

Children's allowances

For children not over 11 on 6th April the allowance is £115 per child.

For children over 11 not over 16 on 6th April the allowance is £140 per child.

For children over 16 undergoing full-time education or training, the allowance is £165 per child.

These allowances are added together and subtracted from the gross income. That which remains is called 'taxable income'. At the moment there is one rate of tax only.

All taxable income is taxed at £0·$38\frac{3}{4}$ ($38\frac{3}{4}$ per cent) in the £.

A full explanation of allowances is given on Form FA1 (1969) Income Tax. Pay As You Earn.

Example

Mr Good earns £27 a week, is married and has three children aged 5, 13 and 18 years. The eldest child is at university. Calculate his taxable income and total tax paid.

Solution

Total salary £27 × 52 = £1404

	£
Allowances	
Earned income allowance $\frac{2}{9}$ × £1404	312
Personal allowance	465
Children's allowances (£115 + £140 + £165)	420
	1197

		£
Taxable income £1404–£1197 = £207		
£207 at $38\frac{3}{4}$p in the £ (i.e. $38\frac{3}{4}$ per cent of £207)		80·21
Taxable income £207	Tax payable	80·21

Note the stages in this calculation.

1. Calculate the total *earnings*—this will include salary, wages, commission and fees, but does not include expenses paid by employers for travelling and meals, or interest from banks and dividends. The first £15 interest on savings bank and similar accounts is tax free, but must be declared to the income tax authorities. Dividends are called 'unearned income' and in most cases are subject to tax at the 'standard rate', i.e. $38\frac{3}{4}$ pence in the £ at the moment.

2. Calculate

a. Earned income allowance—this is *usually* two-ninths of the total earnings (see note on page 15),

b. Personal allowance, and

c. Children's allowances.

Add the allowances together and *subtract* this figure *from* the *total earnings*. This will give the amount on which tax must be paid. It is called the taxable income.

Example
Taxable income £124; find the tax paid.

Solution

$$£124 \text{ at } 38\tfrac{3}{4}\text{p in the } £ = 124 \times £0{\cdot}38\tfrac{3}{4} = \overset{£}{48{\cdot}05}$$

Taxable income £124   Tax payable 48·05

Example
Taxable income £644; find the tax paid.

Solution

$$£644 \text{ at } 38\tfrac{3}{4}\text{p in the } £ = 644 \times £0{\cdot}38\tfrac{3}{4} = 249{\cdot}55$$

Taxable income £644   Tax payable 249·55

Note. Certain amounts are deducted from total earnings before the earned income allowance is calculated. These include superannuation and similar payments, also part of subscriptions to trade and professional organizations.

Example
Earned income £1200, superannuation £72, part of contribution to professional association £3. Calculate earned income allowance.

Solution

Earned income allowance $= \frac{2}{9}$ of (£1200 $-$ £72 $-$ £3)
$= \frac{2}{9}$ of £1125 $=$ £250

Exercises 2A

1. Mr Foster is married, his wife does not work, they have a boy aged 12 and a girl aged 6. His salary is £1 305 per annum.

Mr Styles is a bachelor earning £18 per week.

Miss Brown has an income of £13·50 per week.

Mr Johnson earns £22·50 a week, his wife earns £11·25 a week and they have three sons aged 12, 13 and 15.

Find

a. the annual incomes of Mr Styles, Miss Brown and the Johnson family,

b. the total allowances to which (*i*) Mr Foster; (*ii*) Mr Styles; (*iii*) Miss Brown; (*iv*) Mr Johnson, and (*v*) Mrs Johnson are entitled,

c. the taxable income for each of the above,

d. the amount of tax paid in each case.

2. John Giles, a bachelor, earns £1 650 per year. He pays superannuation at the rate of 6 per cent of his salary per annum. The part of his contribution to his professional organization which is to be deducted from his earnings before his earned income allowance is calculated is £3.

Find

a. his earned income allowance,

b. total allowances,

c. total taxable income,

d. tax paid,

e. net monthly income left after deduction of income tax.

National insurance contributions

Like income tax, these are deducted from your pay before you receive it. Your employer has his share to pay into the scheme also. He buys the appropriate national insurance stamps and affixes them to your national insurance card.

The Department of Health and Social Security issues pamphlets, leaflets and posters giving information about national insurance, current rates of contributions and the benefits obtainable under the scheme.

Find the current rates of contribution in the following cases:

a. employed persons—flat rate contributions;

b. self-employed persons;

c. non-employed persons.

What are the types of benefit offered by the national insurance scheme and how much are these benefits?

Example
Brown, a married man, earns £18 a week and pays 80p national insurance each week. Find his net weekly wage after deductions.

Solution
£18 per week is £936 per annum.

	£
Earned income allowance $\frac{2}{9} \times$ £936 =	208·00
Personal allowance =	465·00
Total allowances =	673·00
Taxable income = £936 − £673 =	263·00

	£
£263 at $38\frac{3}{4}$p in the £ =	101·91
Total tax paid =	101·91

Tax deducted each week $= \dfrac{101·91}{52} = $ £1·96 (approx.)

Weekly wage $=$ £18·00 − £0·80 − £1·96 $=$ £15·24.

Exercises 2B

1. Find the national insurance contributions made by

a. an unemployed youth of 17,

b. an employed woman aged 44 (contracted out of the graduated pension scheme),

c. a self-employed man aged 28,

d. a non-employed woman of 36,

e. an employed man aged 45 earning £24 a week (not contracted out of the graduated pension scheme),

f. the employer of a 17-year-old girl,

g. the employer of a 17-year-old boy,

h. a self-employed woman aged 24,

j. an unemployed girl of 16,

k. the employer of a 26-year-old man (who is not contracted out of the graduated pension scheme and earns £14 per week).

2. Using your table of benefits, find the following:

a. the weekly sickness benefit for a man,

b. the total amount received by

    i. a married man of 45,

    ii. a married woman of 23,

    iii. a girl of 16,

for four weeks' unemployment benefit,

c. the amount received by

    i. a man aged 25,

    ii. a boy aged 16,

    iii. a girl aged 18,

if each person had to be away from work for three weeks due to an injury sustained at work.

d. Find the total amount received in benefits in three months (thirteen weeks) for

    i. an unemployed man with a wife and two children,

    ii. a boy of 17 injured at work,

    iii. an insured married woman, with a child, absent from work ill,

    iv. a widow for the first thirteen weeks of widowhood.

3. Calculate Andrew Hardman's net annual earnings if his gross salary is £1 800 per annum; his national insurance contributions are 89p a week. He is married with a boy of 14 years.

Note. He will pay a graduated pensions contribution.

Superannuation and trade union contributions

The third common deduction from salary is the contribution an employee makes to his own union or association. The amounts vary from trade to trade and from profession to profession.

Find out what you can about

a. local trade union and

b. superannuation contributions.

Who pays these contributions? To whom are they paid? What benefits result from these payments?

Wages and salaries—methods of payment

Cash

Many people prefer to be paid in cash, because the wage is then in a form in which it can be spent immediately. Payment of wages in cash presents certain obvious dangers and problems.

A wages clerk or possibly the employer must first calculate the *gross* wage or earnings of each employee. Then he must deduct income tax, national health contributions and any other accepted amounts, e.g. trade union subscription or pension contributions, which leaves a figure called the *net* wage or earning. This could be an amount such as £13·88. He would then calculate (separately for each wage) the manner in which this amount is to be made up, probably 13 £1 notes, 1 fifty pence coin, 3 ten pence, 1 five pence, 1 two penny and 1 one penny coin.

He may have to repeat this operation many times if there are numerous employees. Consequently having compiled (*a*) the gross wage, (*b*) deductions, (*c*) net wage, (*d*) make-up of net wage, and (*e*) total net wages and their make-up, he needs to take to the bank both a cheque for this total amount and a list of how he requires it.

Example

A firm employs four window-cleaners whose wages and deductions are as shown. Calculate the weekly wage cheque made out by the employer and how the wage packets are made up.

Solution

	Gross wage	PAYE	National insurance	Net wage	£	50p	10p	5p	2p	1p
	£	£	£	£						
A	16·69	2·00	0·81	13·88	13	1	3	1	1	1
B	10·51	1·15	0·81	8·55	8	1		1		
C	7·70	0·30	0·45*	6·95	6	1	4	1		
D	14·73	0·95	0·81	12·97	12	1	4	1	1	
	Weekly wage cheque (A)			42·35	39	4	11	4	2	1

* Under 18 years.

Make-up of wage cheque

$$
\begin{array}{rcl}
 & £ & \\
39 \times £1\cdot00 & = & 39\cdot00 \\
4 \times 50p & = & 2\cdot00 \\
11 \times 10p & = & 1\cdot10 \\
4 \times 5p & = & 0\cdot20 \\
2 \times 2p & = & 0\cdot04 \\
1 \times 1p & = & 0\cdot01 \\
\hline
 & & 42\cdot35 \ (B) \\
\hline
\end{array}
$$

(The two totals A and B must agree)

Exercises 2C

1. Prepare the wage sheet for the following workpeople.

Calculate the net wage for each employee and show how the wage cheque must be made up (i.e. number of £ and 50p, 10p, 5p, etc.) as in the example on page 20.

	Gross wage	PAYE	National insurance	Net wage	£	50p	10p	5p	2p	1p
	£	£	£							
Bell	24·50	3·90	0·81							
Cook	21·00	3·10	0·81							
Dyson	6·40	0·35	0·38							
Evans	6·75	0·40	0·46							
Hall	20·83	2·58	0·64							

The obvious dangers of this method of payment of wages are

a. The clerk, who makes up the wages on the same day of each week, will visit the bank on the same day of each week and probably at approximately the same time. Consequently he runs considerable risk of being attacked and robbed, particularly if he carries very large sums of cash.

b. The employee, who loses a wage packet containing cash, stands little chance of having his money found and returned, whereas other forms of wage payment are of no value except to the person whose name is on the cheque or slip.

Cheque

Payment by cheque involves the wages clerk in slightly less work. He has to calculate the net wage, then write out the cheques and have them signed by the employer. Being paid by cheque means the employee needs an account at a bank to which he can take his cheque and have it exchanged for cash. From the employee's point of view this is sometimes a waste of his time.

Credit transfer

Many salaried people have their salary paid by the employers direct into their personal account. The employer usually informs the employee of the gross amount, net amount and deductions on a small check sheet or slip. This method necessitates the employee having a bank account, but overall is the simplest and safest method of paying wages or salary.

Exercises 2D

Now answer the following questions:

1. What do you understand by the terms:

   a. PAYE,

   b. earned income,

   c. earned income allowance,

   d. personal allowance,

   e. children's allowances,

   f. standard rate of income tax,

   g. trade union contribution,

   h. superannuation?

Find references to some of these terms in the newspaper. Cut them out and use them to illustrate your answer.

2. Find out how wages and salaries are paid in your locality. Comment on the information you have obtained.

3. Obtain all the pamphlets, posters and leaflets giving information about national insurance contributions. What are the benefits of the scheme?

4. Write a short essay on income tax, indicating

   i. the reasons why the allowances are given,

   ii. any lack of fairness in the system, e.g. £375 for a married man, £255 for a widow, and

   iii. how you think the taxation system could be improved.

3 Banks and banking

Banks as we know them today have operated in this country for 150 years. Before that time wealthy people lodged their money with goldsmiths and in return would receive a note which entitled the holder to reclaim his money. Later the goldsmiths found that they had considerable stocks of money and could both lend this money and charge interest on it and also pay interest to the people who had originally deposited money with them, more for security than in the hope of obtaining any benefit.

During the nineteenth century the 'big five' banks began to develop. As the name suggests, these were and still are amongst the most important banks in England. They are:

1. Barclays Bank—first established as a private bank in the eighteenth century. It soon became a union of many private banks, and became a joint stock company in 1896.
2. Lloyds Bank—founded in 1765 in Birmingham, it became a joint stock company in 1865.
3. Midland Bank—established as a joint stock bank in 1836, also in Birmingham, it absorbed many other banks as it grew—one of the largest being the London Joint Stock Bank in 1918.
4. National Provincial Bank—established 1833 and registered as a limited company in 1880.
5. Westminster Bank is an amalgamation of London and Westminster Bank founded 1834 and London and County Bank established 1836—

registered as a limited company in 1880; the amalgamation took place in 1909.

During 1968 there were various mergers between banks. The most noteworthy were

i. between Barclays and Martins Banks—new name Barclays Bank—a further merger with Lloyds was prevented by the Monopolies Commission.

ii. between the National Provincial and Westminster Banks—new name National Westminster Bank.

The Bank Charter Act of 1833 defined the purpose and generally legalized the operations of the joint stock banks.

The Bills of Exchange Act 1882 defined bankers as those whose business related to cheques and other financial documents. The 'paper' side of banking is probably its most striking feature.

It would be quite impossible, and sometimes even dangerous, for everyone who needed to pay others money to carry sufficient cash about with them all the time. Business would be slowed down if cash had to be paid on the spot for goods received and services supplied. Imagine a shop receiving a consignment of electrical goods valued £500 and consider the problems for the shopkeeper of having to have £500 on his premises ready for the arrival of the goods and the huge amounts of money that the delivery men would have to carry back to their works.

The system of payment by cheque overcomes these difficulties and it should be noted that in many cases nowadays shopkeepers receive only a delivery note indicating the nature of the goods delivered; the bill or invoice often comes later. Indeed, whether the invoice is presented at the time of delivery or later, the shopkeeper can pay for his goods at any time by cheque.

However, before a man can write a cheque which a bank will honour (that is pay out the sum indicated) he must have a 'bank account'.

How to open a bank account
The prospective customer usually sees either a cashier or the manager, who will ask him/her for his/her name and address, occupation, and time spent in that employment.

The manager will also ask the customer for references, unless he knows him/her personally.

Having made the acquaintance of the new customer and in due course obtained the references, the manager will ask what sort of account is required. The customer is then asked for a deposit of some sort, either cash or cheque,* and the cashier fills in a paying-in slip (illustrated below) which the customer signs. The cashier then stamps both halves, initials them, and gives the counterfoil to the customer as a receipt.

The bank also requires a specimen signature for records purposes. Upon receipt of the copy of his signature the customer is given a cheque book, for which he can either pay cash or have the cost deducted from his credit balance. He will be asked if crossed or uncrossed cheques are required (see illustration on page 27).

Within a short period of time the customer will be able to cash cheques at the bank and write cheques drawn on his account.

Cheques are usually supplied by banks in books of thirty or sixty and enable a customer (of the bank) with an account to transfer money from his account to anyone else he names.

The preceding paragraphs illustrate two of the most important services that banks render to the community. Firstly, the banks collect and keep

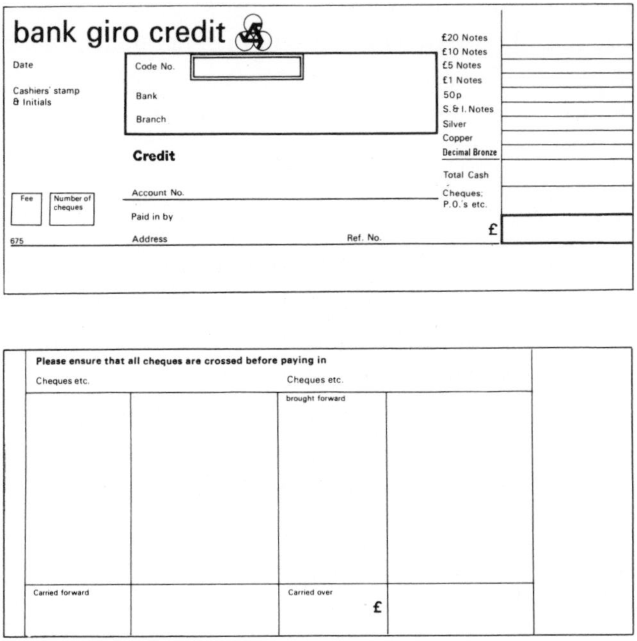
bank giro credit
Date
Cashiers' stamp & Initials
Code No.
Bank
Branch
Credit
Account No.
Paid in by
Address
Ref. No.
Fee
Number of cheques
675
£20 Notes
£10 Notes
£5 Notes
£1 Notes
50p
S. & I. Notes
Silver
Copper
Decimal Bronze
Total Cash
Cheques: P.O.'s etc.
£
Please ensure that all cheques are crossed before paying in
Cheques etc.
Cheques etc.
brought forward
Carried forward
Carried over
£

Fig. 1

* The cheque in this case must be made payable to the prospective customer and drawn on someone else's account.

secure all the surplus monies of people and organizations throughout the country, and secondly they supply cheques which enable their customers to make payments without using cash.

The banks perform yet a third useful service, for they do not allow the money that they have collected to lie idle. Instead they lend this money to other customers who may need money for such things as purchasing goods, building premises or developing a business. The form of lending can be either a loan or an overdraft. Basically an overdraft is permission to draw cheques up to a certain amount when there is no money in the account, creating a debit balance, while a customer receiving a loan is credited with the amount of the loan immediately and repays it at regular intervals. The bank usually requires some security for a loan or overdraft, such as an assurance policy or deeds of a house.

In the cheque illustrated opposite (Fig. 3) Mr Allan Brown, who has signed the cheque, wishes to pay £28·50 to John Watson. The stages in this transaction are as follows:

1. Watson probably supplied goods or services to Brown, who is then in his debt to the extent of £28·50.
2. On or before 20th February (the date on the cheque) Brown has placed at least £28·50 in his own account at the Midland Bank.
3. On 20th February Brown writes the cheque shown and sends it to Watson.
4. Watson pays this into his own bank account.
5. Watson's bank posts it to their own Head Office, who send it via the London Central Clearing House* to the Midland Bank's Head Office, who in turn return it to Brown's branch of the Midland Bank.
6. Watson cannot draw on this cheque until it has been paid by Brown's bank; this usually takes three or four days.
7. Watson's bank increases his account by £28·50 on the day of the receipt. Brown's bank decreases his account by £28·50 on receipt of the cheque through the London Clearing House. No cash has changed hands, only the cheque.

As has been indicated earlier, a cheque is simply a piece of paper which is used to dispense with the need to use cash.

* The Central Clearing House is an institution, in fact a building, established by the banks for the purpose of balancing transactions between the various banks. Most cheques are sent to the respective bank's head offices, sorted and passed through the clearing house and a balance effected between banks. There are some exceptions to this method, such as the local and walks clearings.

Mr Watson is the *payee*—the person to whom the cheque is made payable. The amount is stated both in figures and words.

Mr Brown is the *drawer*—he is the person who has an account with the Midland Bank (5, Mortimer Street, London W1N 8DR Branch), which is the *drawee bank*. It is from this account that the bank will pay the sum of £28·50 to Mr Watson. The drawer must write the amount in words and figures, the date, the name of the payee, and sign the cheque.

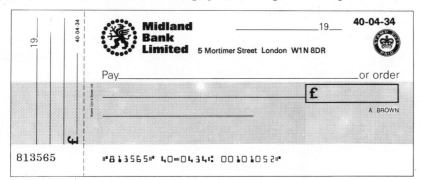

Fig. 2

Fig. 3

Note that at the foot of each cheque there are three sets of numbers printed in electronic characters. The first number is the cheque's individual serial number—this is repeated in ordinary numbers on the cheque counterfoil. The second series of numbers which identifies the bank and branch is repeated in ordinary numbers on the top right-hand corner of the cheque.

Exercises 3A

Either obtain a paying-in slip from the bank or copy the illustration into your books and enter the amounts given in the questions overleaf. Total the paying-in slip and counterfoil.

1. 2 £10 notes, 5 £5 notes, 27 £1 notes, 17 50p pieces, £7·40 silver, £0·81 copper, 2 postal orders £0·74 and £0·62 and cheques from J. Matthews £18·67, W. Johnson £9·48 and L. Price £15·54.

2. 7 £5 notes, 3 £1 notes, 13 50p pieces, £3·55 silver, £0·25 copper, 5 postal orders valued 57p, 62p, 83p, 64p and 71p and cheques from W. Watson £3·76, J. Wrigley £5·18, G. Crook £7·72 and W. Exworth £5·49.

Everyone who makes a payment into a bank account is requested to fill in a paying-in slip. Although the slips may vary in detail, fundamentally they all contain space in which to record on the appropriate lines, precise details of the amount to be paid in. The customer makes a copy of the slip —this is the left-hand side of the perforated slip shown on page 25.

The bank clerk stamps and initials both the slip and the counterfoil and returns the counterfoil to the customer, who keeps it as a record and receipt of the transaction. Later the total can be checked against the entry on the statement or passbook. People who make regular payments can obtain a book of paying-in slips from the bank and this prevents the odd loose slip from getting lost.

To describe all the facilities offered by banks would take many pages, so here follow a number of important points which you should learn.

Types of account
A customer can 'open' a bank account by depositing any sum from 5p upwards. However, certain banks stipulate a minimum opening amount. Accounts with cheque-book facilities fall into two main categories

1. Current, and
2. Personal Cheque Accounts. (This service has been suspended.)

Current accounts
This type of account pays no interest. The customer is charged for the bank's services; these are called bank charges* and are calculated:

 a. on the value of cheques drawn during a half-year, or
 b. on the number of transactions involved during this period, or
 c. by discussion between bank and customer in the case of large accounts.

* Some customers pay no bank charges when they maintain an agreed minimum credit balance in their account.

Personal cheque accounts
These were introduced by the Midland Bank in September 1958. They were designed primarily for people who wish to use the bank *only* for the deposit and withdrawal of money and the facility of having a cheque book. Each cheque costs $2\frac{1}{2}$p, which includes stamp duty and commission on each cheque; there are no further charges and a customer may not overdraw his account. (This service has been suspended.)

Deposit accounts
These usually pay interest at a rate 2 per cent below the Bank Rate. The minimum deposit is £1 and withdrawal can only be made when the agreed notice is given (usually seven days). Cheques are not used with this sort of account. The state of the account is shown in the customer's passbook.

Savings accounts
Originally, these involved the use of a home-safe. At present interest at $3\frac{1}{2}$ per cent is paid on the first £250 and thereafter at the deposit account rate and the state of the account is shown in the passbook. Cheques are not issued with these accounts, but a person may present his passbook at *any* branch and ask for sums up to £10.

The bank statement
The state of some bank accounts is shown on a statement, and in other cases it is found in a passbook.

It will be noted that both statement and passbook contain essentially the same information, namely a record of all the money paid into and out of the accounts.

Examine the three statements and note the following points:
1. The name of the customer is shown at the top of each sheet.
2. The name and branch of the bank is printed immediately below this.
3. The date of each transaction is shown.
4. In the case of withdrawals from the account each item is identified either by words, letters or numbers. All abbreviations are explained by a printed footnote on the statement. The numbers are usually the last three serial numbers of the cheque.
5. Payments into the account are also identified, by the words cash, cheques or sundries, but occasionally special letters or words are used to denote salary payment. These letters or words indicate the name of the person paying the salary into the account.
6. The balance is recorded after each transaction.

Example of a bank statement

Beverly Ford, Esq,

In account with the . . . . Bank Limited . . . . Branch

33 High Street, ... Lancashire

1969	*Debit*			*Credit*		*Balance*	*Credit** *Overdrawn OD*
			£		£		£
May 23							136·14*
May 24		378	10·00				126·14*
May 28		380	73·25				52·89*
May 30				LCC	146·62		199·51*
June 1	SO		3·72				195·79*
June 8		379	67·99				127·80*
June 29				LCC	148·12		275·92*
June 30	CHS		2·62				273·30*
July 4		521	41·44				231·86*
July 5				Personal Loan	250·00		481·86*
July 8		522	450·00				31·86*

CHS Charges on A/c	DIV Dividend	INT Interest	SO Standing Order
	DO Ditto	SDS Sundries	UPD Unpaid

Note. An overdrawn or debit balance is shown in red, except when a branch is computer-serviced when both credit balances and overdrafts are shown in black.

Exercises 3B

Answer these questions using the statement shown above.

1. What was the balance at the start of the series of transactions?
2. What was the balance at the end of this period?
3. What was the balance on
   a. 30th May,
   b. 8th June,
   c. 3rd July?
4. What could the letters L.C.C. stand for?
5. What are the payments £146·62, £148·12 into Ford's account?
6. What do the abbreviations SO and CHS stand for?

Example of a deposit account passbook

DEPOSIT ACCOUNT

Name . . . .

in account, with . . . . Bank Limited . . . . Branch

Subject to notice of withdrawal as notified

Date		Withdrawn	Lodged	Balance
1969		£	£	£
May 23	Balance b/f			136·14
May 24	Cash	10·00		126·14
May 28	Cash	73·25		52·89
May 30	LCC		146·62	199·51
June 1	SO	3·72		195·79
June 8	Cash	67·99		127·80
June 30	Interest		2·60	130·40
June 30	LCC		148·12	278·52
July 4	Dividends		17·81	296·33

Exercises 3C

Here is a collection of bank transactions which occurred during the period November 1965 to January 1966:

		£
	Credit balance on November 16	144·86
Nov 17	Howard paid electricity account	17·97
18	Housekeeping expenses	44·00
20	Cheque from Inland Revenue	6·74
24	Howard paid rates	45·43
Dec 2	Standing order—insurance	3·83
9	Howard paid telephone bill	9·64
10	Paid in cash	7·35
21	Drew cash for Christmas expenses	25·00
23	Salary	119·73
Jan 3	Standing order—insurance	3·83

1. Record these transactions in Thomas Howard's deposit account passbook in the form illustrated above. Indicate whether there is a credit or debit balance at the end of the year.

2. Using the above information, show Thomas Howard's statement in the form illustrated; include the following item:

Dec 31st   bank charges £2·65

Example of a savings account passbook

SAVINGS ACCOUNT

.... Bank Limited

.... Branch

Name........................

Address........................ Signature................

Date	Amount in words	With-drawn	Lodged	Balance	Bank stamp
1969		£	£	£	
May 23	One hundred and thirty-six pounds fourteen			136·14	
May 24	Ten pounds	10·00		126·14	
May 28	Seventy-three pounds twenty-five	73·25		52·89	
June 7	Thirty-five pounds seventy-six		35·76	88·65	
			Carried forward	88·65	

3. Divide the following items into debit items (charges on the account) and credit items (payments into the account) in William Jones's account with the Midland Bank:

Oct 9th self £63; Oct 11th salary £114; Oct 17th cash and cheques £47·50; Oct 19th sundries £16; Oct 20th S.E. Gas Board £13·63.

4. Assuming that Jones started this period with a credit balance of £23, find his balance after the above transactions had taken place.

5. The address of the bank is 8 Lord Street, Stanchester. Draw up a statement from the bank showing the transactions in Question 3.

6. What are the most important services rendered by the banks?

7. Describe the types of account a customer may open with a bank. Indicate points of similarity and difference.

8. When a customer opens an account the bank requires copies of his signature. For what purpose are these required?

9. Describe the different methods used by banks to record the state of a customer's account.

10. By means of sketches indicate what a cheque looks like and what essential information must always be written or printed on it.

11. Name the different types of cheque and say what the difference is and what these differences mean.

12. In what circumstances does a bank not make payment on a customer's cheque?

13. Explain the difference between an order and a bearer cheque.

14. What is the purpose and value to an ordinary citizen of being able to use cheques both to make and accept payments?

15. What is meant by endorsing a cheque and why is this done?

16. Describe the full range of operations associated with the life of a single cheque starting at the moment when a customer first obtains it over the counter of a bank.

17. What is the difference between a bank loan and an overdraft?

18. How does a bank make money
a. from a customer with a deposit account?
b. from a customer with a current account?

19. Are there any other ways by which a bank makes money?

20. a. What were the 'Big Five'? *b.* What are the 'Big Four'? Discuss the change.

21. What is a bank? Discuss this question and indicate what service it renders to the community.

22. What is a clearing house?

23. Explain the meaning of:

a. interest
b. current account
c. crossed cheque
d. statement
e. deposit account
f. open cheque
g. passbook
h. overdraft
j. bank loan
k. bank charges
l. referred to drawer
m. 'heel, 'stub' or counterfoil of a cheque
n. paying-in slip.

24. Find out some of the different words that can be written between the parallel lines of a crossing on a cheque and write down their meaning.

25. What is the difference between the various sets of numbers at the top and bottom of a cheque?

26. Describe in short sentences the main functions of a bank.

27. Draw and describe the more important bank documents.

28. Inquire from the bank about other services not mentioned in this chapter and write a short account of three of these services.

Savings banks

Savings banks were first suggested by Daniel Defoe in 1697, but the first one established in England was in 1799 by Rev. Joseph Smith at Wendover. In 1817 legislation had become necessary because of the growth and importance of savings banks.

The financial Acts of Parliament of that time stated that the management of each bank must be carried out by unpaid trustees who made regular reports to the Government and invested all their funds in government stock.

During the next fifty years the number of savings banks increased—there were 622 in 1863—but from that time on, partly due to the start of the Post Office Savings Bank, which seemed to offer depositors greater security, and also due to the general decrease in popularity and security of private banks the number of savings banks decreased. (See National Savings Bank, page 47.)

How to use your savings bank

The passbook or bankbook is always required whenever any business is to be transacted.

1. If you wish to *deposit* money then, like any other bank, you fill in a paying-in slip as shown below, sign it and hand it to the clerk with your passbook, in which is recorded every transaction. Any sums, large or small, not exceeding £5000 in total may be deposited.

Account No. . . . . £ _____

Please Credit the items specified overleaf.

Signature . . . .

. . . . Trustee Savings Bank

Fig. 4

Cheques	Amount		£
Name	£	£10 Bank Notes	
		£5 ,, ,,	
		£1 , ,,	
		50 pence	
		Silver (not 50p)	
		Bronze/Copper	
Total cheques c/f		Total cash	
		Total cheques b/f	
		Total Credit	

Fig. 5 The above information is printed on the reverse side of a paying-in slip.

2. Compound interest is paid on savings banks' ordinary accounts at the rate of $3\frac{1}{2}$ per cent per annum. This is calculated monthly on a particular day of each month and entered annually in your passbook.

3. Withdrawals are made by filling-in a withdrawal form, signing it and handing it to the bank clerk with your passbook.

Note. This is one major difference between a Trustee Savings Bank and a Joint Stock Bank.

Account No.	£
Received from the Trustees of the . . . . Trustee Savings Bank the above amount.	
Depositor	
By cash cheque payable to . . . . Trustee Savings Bank	

Fig. 6

The passbook of a general department Trustee Savings Bank Account is very similar to other bank statements. Note that special items like interest and standing orders carry identification letters and that the balance is shown after every transaction.

A typical page of a passbook is now shown:

Branch   . . . . Trustee Savings Bank
No. 7272   Mr John K. Williams

	Deposits		Withdrawals	Date	Balance
	£		£		£
				Nov 13 '70	34·21
	3·50			Nov 16 '70	37·71
IN	0·28			Nov 20 '70	37·99
			7·58	Nov 28 '70	30·41
			17·85	Dec 4 '70	12·56
		SO	2·15	Jan 8 '71	10·41
CQ	18·42			Jan 17 '71	28·83
	45·50			Jan 30 '71	74·33
			8·73	Feb 6 '71	65·60
			55·00	Feb 16 '71	10·60
TS	78·00			Apr 3 '71	88·60
CQ	107·13			Apr 4 '71	195·73
		CQ	190·00	Apr 5 '71	5·73

SO	Standing Order		PS	Purchase of Stock
IN	Interest		SS	Sale of Stock
DV	Dividend		TS	Transfer Special I.D.
CQ	Cheque		TO	Transfer other S. Bank

Exercises 3D

1. Record the following items as they would appear in a general department Trustee Savings Bank passbook. Balance on March 30th £105·30.
Deposits April 1st £19·50; April 4th £25·80;
          April 10th £19·42; April 11th £15·33;
          April 17th £33·48; April 24th £45·00.
Cash withdrawals April 5th £50·00; April 12th £30·00;
                April 19th £20·00; April 26th £30·00.
Interest April 18th £4·49.
Standing Order April 12th £14·25.

2. Record twelve items in a Trustee Savings Bank passbook which might occur during one month. Include payments of interest and standing orders.

Special investment department

A customer with a credit balance of £50 in his general department account may open special investment department accounts which pay compound interest at the rates of 7 and 6 per cent per annum calculated as stated earlier. The bank usually asks for three or one month's notice respectively before any sum is withdrawn from these accounts.

An extract from a special investment department passbook is shown below. You will notice that the balance is shown below each transaction.

Date		Amount £	
1970			
Mar 3	Deposit	26·00	OY
May 5	Deposit	17·00	KB
		43·00	
May 19	Deposit	34·00	OY
		77·00	
June 11	Paid	42·00	OY
		35·00	

Exercises 3E

1. Record the following items in a Trustee Savings Bank special investment department passbook.
Balance on 25th October 1970 £425·00.
Deposits 26th October £73·00;   5th November £41·27;
            15th November £18·90; 4th December £5·63.
Withdrawals 28th October £156·20;   19th November £121·10;
            21st November £50·62.
Interest 20th November £12·30.

2. Describe some of the differences between a general department passbook and a special investment department passbook.

3. If a depositor wishes to withdraw cash from the Trustee Savings Bank he does not use a cheque. Comment on the difference between withdrawing money at a Trustee Savings Bank and at a Joint Stock Bank, e.g. Barclays, Lloyds, Midland.
   a. from a customer's point of view, and
   b. from the bank's point of view.

4 Post Office services

The Post Office offers a wide variety of services not only to the general public but also to industry and commerce.

The principal services are:

a. Inland postal service.
b. Inland telegraph and telephone services.
c. Inland remittance and savings services.
d. The above services but to the Irish Republic (except Savings).
e. Overseas post and air mail services.
f. Overseas telegraph and telephone services.
g. Overseas remittance services.
h. Sale of non-postage stamps, licences, national insurance stamps, etc.

Inland postal service

As the charges for letters, postcards and parcels and the fees for registration and recorded delivery are changed occasionally by the Post Office, no charges or fees will be shown in this section.

Go to your local post office and make the following inquiries:

a. What is the system of postal charges for
    i. letters?
    ii. postcards?
    iii. parcels?

b. Is there a limit to the size or weight of
  i. a letter?
  ii. a postcard?
  iii. a parcel?
c. Find out what *registration* means. What are the charges?
d. What is *recorded delivery*? How much does it cost?

Exercises 4A

Using the information you have obtained about the inland postal services, answer the following questions.

1. Find the charge for sending the following by *letter post*. Which of them are outside the limits imposed by the Post Office?
  a. a small letter weighing 14 g,
  b. a small letter weighing 42 g,
  c. a small letter weighing 0·1 kg,
  d. a package 51 cm × 51 cm × 46 cm weighing 1·36 kg.
  e. another package 53 cm × 43 cm × 30 cm weighing 1·81 kg,
  f. a roll 51 cm long and 10 cm diameter weighing 0·51 kg,
  g. a roll 71 cm long and 15 cm diameter weighing 0·6 kg,
  h. a roll 0·9144 m long and 2·54 cm diameter weighing 0·26 kg?

2. What would be the total cost of buying and sending 48 postcards, 12 of which were 15 cm × 10 cm and cost 3p each, the remainder being 13 cm × 8 cm and cost $2\frac{1}{2}$p each?

3. Find the cost of sending parcels whose weights are as follows:
a. 7·71 kg, *b.* 1·36 kg, *c.* 2·5 kg, *d.* 9·5 kg, *e.* 8·6 kg.

4. Certain of the following items would not be accepted by the Post Office for transmission by the method shown. Select these and give the reason for your selection. The first one is worked for you.

Item	*Size*	*Weight*	*Method of delivery*	*Reason*
Parcel	0·5 m × 0·45 m × 0·4 m	11 kg	Parcel post	11 kg exceeds the weight limit of 10 kg for parcels
a. Parcel	1·3 m × 0·3 m × 0·1 m	4 kg	Parcel post	
b. Letter	0·1 m × 0·08 m	0·10 kg	Recorded delivery letter post	
c. Package	1 m × 0·3 m × 0·15 m	3 kg	Recorded delivery letter post	
d. Package	1 m × 0·3 m × 0·15 m	3 kg	Parcel post	
e. Card	0·4 m × 0·1 m	3 g	Letter post	

f. Parcel	0·4 m × 0·3 m × 1 m	4 kg	Recorded delivery parcel post
g. Package	0·1 m × 0·1 m × 0·03 m (value £18)	3 kg	Registered post parcel post
h. Package	1 m × 1 m × 0·3 m (value £57)	2 kg	Registered post

Calculate the cost of posting those items which would be accepted by the Post Office.

5. Find out all you can about express mail services. Who uses this service and when is it used?

6. If you had travelled from Liverpool to London on your way to the Continent via Dover and found you had left your passport at home, describe the steps you would take to have it sent to you at Dover by the fastest possible service.

Inland telegraph and telephone services

Inquire at your local post office, or use your *Post Office Guide* if it is up-to-date to find the cost of sending a telegram. Make sure you know the difference between an 'ordinary' and a 'greetings' telegram.

Handing in a telegram

By hand. A telegram should be written in *block* capitals and handed in at any post office or railway station which does telegraph business.

By telephone. A telegram may be dictated at any time from a subscriber's telephone or from a public call office.

Counting for charging

The address. The words in the name and address as well as those in the message are all counted for charging purposes subject to the exceptions listed in this section. All the necessary words in an address after the name of the road, street and so on are charged for as one word. Telephone and telex addresses are charged for as two words, excluding the name of the addressee.

Names of towns (Southend-on-Sea), compound names (De la Rue), words normally coupled by hyphens (mother-in-law) and abbreviations in general use (can't) are all charged for as single words.

When figures and letters are mixed they must be counted separately; for example, Ab4d is charged for as three words and 1197A is charged for as two words.

House numbers which include letters, for example 209A, are charged for as one word.

A sign (hyphen, full stop), a bar in a fraction and an oblique line all count as one figure; for example $2\frac{3}{4}$ counts as four figures, 2% counts as four figures. Exceptionally, although they consist of letters and the equivalent of figures, abbreviations in general use, for example, a/c and c/o count as one word each.

Underlining. When words are underlined, or placed in brackets or inverted commas, each underlining, pair of brackets or set of inverted commas is charged for as one word.

Exercises 4B

1. What would it cost to send the following telegrams:

Type	Number of words	Day or date
Ordinary	16	Wednesday
Ordinary	10	Thursday
Greetings standard	15	Tuesday
Ordinary	24	Sunday
Greetings—de luxe	19	Friday
Overnight	20	Wednesday
Ordinary	16	Christmas Day
Ordinary—prepaid reply	20, Reply 16 words	Tuesday

2. Find the cost of sending the following telegrams:

a. JONES 14 MILLBANK STREET STOCKPORT ARRIVING LIVERPOOL SATURDAY 11 A.M. JACK

b. COMBRAY PRODUCTS HILLS ROAD LEAGATE BRISTOL SEND SPECIAL GEARBOX IMMEDIATELY ROGERS GOODWOOD GARAGE

c. MR & MRS MELLOW 17 HEAVITREE ROAD HASTINGS HAPPY ANNIVERSARY ALL GOOD WISHES FOR FUTURE HEALTH WEALTH AND HAPPINESS TOM AND GEORGE

d. JACOBS DOVER ROAD NEWPORT PAGNELL GOLDGERG UNABLE TO HELP SEND INSTRUCTIONS AND CASH MISSION PROBABLY SUCCESSFUL SOLOMON

3. Will the Post Office accept a telegram written in code?

4. Who else besides a post office may accept a telegram for transmission?

Telephone service

Exchange line service

Rentals range from £4 to £6* a quarter according to the service provided. Connexion charges are payable. Accounts are rendered quarterly.

Public call offices

A higher scale of charges is payable to cover the use of the call office. Call offices are available to the general public throughout the country, most of them continuously day and night.

Connexion charges

A connexion charge (£25 maximum) is payable in respect of each exchange line. Where an existing installation is taken over without alteration or change of telephone number no charge is made.

Connexion charges for internal extensions vary from £2 to £5; for external extensions from £5 to £50.

Call charges

Great Britain, Northern Ireland, Channel Islands and Isle of Man. Calls to exchanges outside the local call areas are known as trunk calls. For the calculations of trunk-call charges exchanges are grouped, and a central point in each group is used for the measurement of chargeable distance.

Call charges with subscriber trunk dialling (STD)

Where subscriber trunk dialling facilities are available, local and dialled trunk calls are charged in units of 1p (2p for calls from pay-on-answer coin-box lines) for periods of time depending on the time and chargeable distance of the call. (See *Post Office Guide* for additional information.)

Local calls (from STD Exchanges)

Ordinary lines: Time bought for 1p.
           Monday to Friday 08.00 to 18.00 .... 6 minutes
           Monday to Friday 18.00 to 08.00 and all
               day Saturday and Sunday .... 12 minutes
Coinbox lines: Time bought for 2p.
           Monday to Friday 08.00 to 18.00 .... 3 minutes
           Monday to Friday 18.00 to 08.00 and all
               day Saturday and Sunday .... 6 minutes

* Business rate—exclusive £6, shared £5.
   Residence rate—exclusive £5, shared £4.

Inland Trunk Calls—Dialled Direct   Time bought for 1p (STD)

Distance in km	Peak Rate	Standard Rate	Cheap Rate
	Monday–Friday 09.00–12.00	Monday–Friday 08.00–09.00 12.00–18.00	Every night 18.00–08.00 and all day Sat/Sun
up to 55	20 seconds	30 seconds	72 seconds
55 to 80	12 seconds	15 seconds	36 seconds
over 80	8 seconds	10 seconds	36 seconds

Inland Trunk Calls connected by the Operator

3 minute call—minimum charge (each subsequent minute or part thereof at $\frac{1}{3}$ rate shown)

Distance in km	Peak Rate	Standard Rate	Intermediate Rate*	Cheap Rate*
	Monday–Friday 09.00–12.00	Monday–Friday 08.00–09.00 12.00–18.00	Saturday 08.00–18.00	Every night 18.00–08.00 and all day Sunday
	p	p	p	p
up to 55	$10\frac{1}{2}$	9	6	3
55 to 80	18	$13\frac{1}{2}$	9	6
over 80	$25\frac{1}{2}$	$22\frac{1}{2}$	15	9

Coinbox lines

Inland Trunk Calls—Dialled Direct   Time bought for 2p (STD)

Distance in km	Standard Rate	Cheap Rate
	Monday–Friday 08.00–18.00	Every night 18.00–08.00 and all day Sat/Sun
up to 55	30 seconds	90 seconds
55 to 80	24 seconds	45 seconds
over 80	15 seconds	45 seconds

* These cheap rates are suspended on certain public holidays.

Inland Trunk Calls connected by the Operator

3 minute call minimum charge and each subsequent 3-minute period

Distance in km	Standard Rate	Intermediate Rate*	Cheap Rate*
	Monday–Friday 08.00–18.00	Saturday 08.00–18.00	Every night 18.00–08.00 and all day Sunday
	p	p	p
up to 55	16	10	6
55 to 80	20	16	10
over 80	26	20	12

* These cheap rates are suspended on certain public holidays.

Call charges where STD is not available

Local calls. The charge for a call from a subscriber's line (without a coin box) to another line on any exchange within the local call area is $1\frac{1}{2}$p if made from a business line or residence line and 2p if made from a coinbox line. These calls are untimed.

Trunk calls. Trunk calls are charged at the rates given on page 43 for calls via the operator.

Public call offices

Telephone kiosks and other types of call offices are available in all parts of the country for the general public to make telephone calls and to dictate telegrams.

Call charges

A charge is made for a local (untimed) call from a call office or coin-box line where STD is not available.

The charges for trunk calls made via the operator also apply to trunk calls made from call offices except that after the first period of three minutes calls are normally charged for in three-minute periods.

An additional charge to the trunk-call charge is made for a trunk call from a call office.

Transferred charge calls

The charge for a call from any telephone may be debited on request to the called subscriber, if the latter or the person answering the called telephone agrees to accept it. The request must be made at the time the call is booked.

Personal calls
A call may be booked as a personal call on payment of a small extra charge.
  A personal call enables a caller to

  a. quote the name of the person to whom he wishes to speak and the names of any acceptable substitutes and the telephone numbers or addresses where all or any of them may be found;
  b. specify the person to whom he wishes to speak by a reference code, title or department or by an extension number, for example 469/BUY/2; Sales Department; General Manager; Extension 123;
  c. arrange to speak only if two named persons are both available at one particular number;
  d. arrange for a person, not on the telephone, to be brought to a neighbour's telephone whose number he gives.

  If the personal call cannot be completed at once the originating exchange operator will *leave word* at the distant telephone for the wanted person to ring the personal-call operator at the calling exchange as soon as possible. The call is then connected. Alternatively, either the caller or the called number may give the time at which further attempt(s) should be made to obtain the wanted person or they may quote another number at which he may be found.
  Personal calls, if not previously completed, are cancelled twenty-four hours after the time of booking.
  The small extra charge payable for the above service is known as the personal fee and is the same whatever the distance or duration of the call. This charge becomes payable as soon as an inquiry has been made of any distant number quoted by the caller, whether the call has been effective or not, but only one fee is payable irrespective of the number of attempts made to complete the call.
  The timing of a call does not start until connexion has been made to the person required, or to an acceptable substitute if the caller decides to speak to someone else at the called or alternative numbers. If the required person or acceptable substitutes cannot be traced, only the personal fee is payable.

Exercises 4C
  1. Mr Brown wished to have a telephone installed in his house. What is

the installation of a telephone likely to cost and how much rent will he have to pay if he intends to use it for social and domestic purposes?

2. What is meant by 'shared service'? By how much does the rental for a shared-service connexion differ from an 'exclusive' connexion? What is the quarterly rent

a. for business use

b. for domestic use?

3. What is the difference between a local and a trunk call?

4. A man used a private telephone with STD service to make the following calls. How much did each call cost?

Type of call	Distance in km	Duration of call	Time	Day
a. Local		5 min	11.30	Wednesday
b. Local		7 min	19.30	Thursday
c. Local		11 min	15.20	Friday
d. Local		18 min	15.20	Sunday
e. Trunk	72	3 min 10 s	07.15	Monday
f. Trunk	40	2 min 45 s	06.30	Tuesday
g. Trunk	160	3 min	23.30	Tuesday
h. Trunk	64	1 min 30 s	19.45	Saturday
j. Trunk	96	5 min	11.30	Tuesday
k. Trunk	40	3 min 40 s	07.15	Sunday
l. Trunk via operator	39	6 min	16.30	Tuesday
m. Trunk via operator	75	4 min 27 s	18.40	Friday
n. Trunk via operator	104	9 min 15 s	22.00	Wednesday
o. Trunk via operator	193	2 min 40 s	10.30	Sunday
p. Trunk via operator	385	1 min 30 s	12.15	Tuesday
q. Trunk via operator	85	5 min 8 s	12.30	Christmas Day
r. Trunk via operator	111	3 min 30 s	20.00	Good Friday
s. Trunk via operator	47	5 min 12 s	04.30	Tuesday
t. Trunk via operator	78	8 min 5 s	06·40	Friday
u. Trunk via operator	106	4 min	09.15	Monday
v. Trunk via operator	128	1 min	10.30	Saturday
w. Trunk via operator	241	5 min	18.30	Tuesday

5. What would each of the calls cost in Question 4 if they had been made from a public call office or coin-box with STD pay-on-answer facilities?

6. What would each of the calls cost in Question 4 if they were made from a private subscriber's premises not equipped with STD?

7. If the charges for the trunk calls via the operator in Question 4 were transferred to the called subscriber (often called reversing the charge), what would have been the total cost of these calls?

8. Describe what is meant by a personal call. Illustrate your answer with an example and indicate the range of inquiries that an operator will undertake in connexion with a personal call.

Inland remittance and savings services

Inland remittance services

These Post Office services provide a convenient means of transferring money by post. There are two types of remittance—the postal order and the money order.

Use your *Post Office Guide* or find out from the Post Office about *postal orders* and *money orders*. Write out this information in your own words.

Exercises 4D

Find the cost, including poundage, of the following:

1. Postal orders costing: *a.* 11p, *b.* 16p, *c.* 24p, *d.* 31p, *e.* 60p, *f.* 72p, *g.* £1·31, *h.* £3·52, *j.* £4·97.

2. Money orders costing: *a.* 16p, *b.* 72p, *c.* £1·31, *d.* £3·52, *e.* £4·97, *f.* £14·97, *g.* £23·85, *h.* £32·41, *j.* £46·71.

National Savings Bank

In common with other savings banks, the National Savings Bank pays interest to people who put their savings in the Post Office. Such people are called *depositors* and they each have a book called a *bank-book* which records amounts paid in—*deposits*—and amounts taken out—*withdrawals*. Depositors are advised to send their books to the head office once each year so that the interest can be entered. Interest is a sum of money credited to depositors in return for putting their savings in the Post Office and the amount varies with the size of the deposit and the length of time it is left in the account.

Interest is calculated at the rate of $2\frac{1}{2}$ per cent per annum per complete £ for complete months only.

Therefore, if £100 was deposited for 12 months, the interest would be £2·50.

So if £1 was deposited for 12 months the interest would be $£\frac{2 \cdot 50}{100}$ or $2\frac{1}{2}$p

and if £1 was deposited for 1 month the interest would be $\frac{2\frac{1}{2}}{12}$p or $\frac{5}{24}$p.

It should be noted that interest is only given on whole pounds which have been in the account for complete calendar months. If a depositor already had £12 in an account on the first of a month and did not withdraw it during that month he would be entitled to $12 \times \frac{5}{24}$p interest, i.e. $2\frac{1}{2}$p.

Exercises 4E
1. Work out the interest due on these accounts:
   a. £9 for 4 months,
   b. £10 for 6 months,
   c. £14 for 6 months,
   d. £40 for 9 months.

Example

A man opens this account on 3rd February and fills one page of his National Savings Bank-book by 17th February.

Below is shown the next page of his National Savings Bank-book. Note how the amount of each deposit is written in words as well as in figures. Calculate the interest due each month and the total interest due to the end of June.

Date of deposit or Warrant, etc.	Amount of deposit in words or method of withdrawal	Deposit £	Withdrawal £
Balance (not exceeding) 1970	Eighteen pounds	17·76	
March 24	Four pounds, seventy-three	4·73	
April 2	Demand		4·00
April 8	One pound, fifty-five	1·55	
May 5	Demand		5·50
May 16	Three pounds, fifty	3·50	
June 2	Warrant		7·00

Solution

The balance must be found after each transaction.

Date	Deposit	Withdrawal	Balance
1970	£	£	£
February 17 (Balance)	17·76		17·76
March 24	4·73		22·49
April 2		4·00	18·49
April 8	1·55		20·04
May 5		5·50	14·54
May 16	3·50		18·04
June 2		7·00	11·04

Interest in pence is calculated as follows:
Number of complete pounds in bank account during the whole month times $2\frac{1}{2}$ divided by 12.

Month	Lowest credit balance in £'s	Number of complete £'s
February	0·00	0
March	17·76	17
April	18·49	18
May	14·54	14
June	11·04	11
		60

Total interest due to the end of June $= 60p \times 2\frac{1}{2} \div 12 = 12\frac{1}{2}p$.

To find the lowest balance, find the balance after every transaction.

Note
   i. that the account was only opened in February, so there can be no interest for February;
   ii. that the figure £17·76 is the lowest credit balance from 17th February to 24th March and is therefore the lowest credit balance in March.

Deposits
Cash, cheques, savings stamps, gift tokens, postal and money orders, may be deposited providing that not less than 25p is tendered.

Withdrawals
Up to £20 is payable on demand, but the Post Office retains the book when more than one withdrawal on demand over £3 is made in any period of seven days. Not more than one withdrawal on demand is permitted in any one day. Larger amounts can be withdrawn by giving notice. Four days for cash deposits and eight days for cheque deposits must elapse before a deposit is withdrawn, excluding Sundays, holidays and the days of deposit and withdrawal.

Crossed warrants
These warrants, similar to cheques and only payable through a bank account, are available on application by a depositor. Crossed warrants are not issued for amounts of less than £1.

Exercises 4F

1. Which of the following may be deposited in the National Savings Bank:

    a. Notes and coins value £3·65.

    b. A postal order for 61p.

    c. Fourteen American dollars value £5 approximately.

    d. A money order for £4·50.

    e. A book of national savings stamps value £1·10.

    f. A cheque for £8·80.

    g. A single national savings stamp value $2\frac{1}{2}$p.

    h. A collection of twenty-one new halfpennies.

    j. An opening deposit of 20p?

2. Indicate whether all the transactions in the following examples are permitted by the Post Office:

    a. Credit balance £28, withdrawal on demand of £3 on February 4th.

    b. Credit balance £28, withdrawals on demand of £3 on February 4th, 5th, 6th and 7th.

    c. Credit balance £28, withdrawals on demand of £3 February 6th, £5 February 7th and £10 February 8th.

    d. Credit balance £28, withdrawals on demand of £3 February 6th, £10 February 6th, £5 February 7th, £3 February 8th.

    e. Credit balance £28, withdrawal on demand £15 October 8th.

    f. Credit balance £28, withdrawal on demand £5 October 12th, and withdrawal giving notice £17 October 24th.

    g. Credit balance £2, deposit cheque £7 October 4th; withdrawal on demand £8 October 5th.

    h. Credit balance £5, deposit cheque £15 September 5th; withdrawal giving notice £20 September 15th.

3. What is the minimum amount for which a crossed warrant is issued?

4. If a balance of £145 had been in an account since the beginning of 1970 and no further transactions took place during that year, how much would the interest be on this account for 1970?

Date of deposit or warrant, etc.	Amount of deposit in words or method of withdrawal	Deposits £	Withdrawals £	Initials	Date stamp
Balance (not exceeding)	Two pounds	1·22		JM	
1970					
June 16	Twenty-two pounds	22·00		RL	
Aug 3	On demand		4·00	AY	
Aug 16	On demand		3·00	RL	
Aug 19	On demand		3·00	JM	
Nov 6	Cheque, Four pounds twenty	4·20		AY	
Nov 8	Warrant		15·00	JM	
Nov 25	Twenty-five pence	0·25		RL	
	Totals	27·67	25·00		

Depositors are requested to examine all entries before leaving the Post Office.

A page of a National Savings Bank-book is shown above. If the balance of £1·22 had been in the account since 31st December 1969, what would be (a) the interest due on this account on 31st December 1970, and (b) the total balance in the account?

6. Using the bank-book shown on page 48.

a. What is the balance on the 1st of March, April, May and June?

b. Find the interest to be added for the three months, July, August, and September, if the following transactions take place:
Deposits: 5th July £12·50; 19th August £15; 2nd September £3·26.
Withdrawals: 9th July £10; 3rd September £7.

c. If no further deposits or withdrawals were made during the year, find the balance on 31st December before interest is added.

d. Find the interest due from 17th February to 31st December.

e. Calculate the total balance in the account including interest on 31st December.

National savings certificates
Savings certificates were first issued on 21st February 1916.

These can be purchased from the Post Office and banks either for cash or by cheque. At post offices they can be obtained in exchange for national savings stamps which are often sold in schools. Since they were introduced in 1916 there have been several issues of savings certificates of various values ranging from 50p to £1 and maturing over different periods of time. For instance, a recent issue is the eleventh (11th) issue of national savings certificates. The 11th issue cost £1 each unit and are worth £1·25 after 6 years. Certificates were sold in 1, 2, 3, 4, 5, 10, 20, 50, 100 and 200 pound units, but no one person may hold more than 600 units. A more recent issue (the 12th) of savings certificates cost £1 each and are worth £1·25 after 5 years. No person may hold more than 500 units.

Interest on national savings certificates is free of income tax and surtax. The rate of interest varies from year to year and generally speaking improves as the certificate approaches its maturing value.

Certificates may be kept for a period after maturity and full details of their value and of the maximum permitted holding may be obtained from the Post Office on form Savings Certificates P156H.

The possible growth of a £1 certificate is shown in the table below and indicates the price paid to the holder if repayment is required.

Special issue
Rate of growth month by month

On comple-tion of	1st year	2nd year	3rd year	4th year	5th year	6th year
	£	£	£	£	£	£
1st month	1·00	1·02	1·05	1·08	1·13	1·19
2nd month	1·00	1·02	1·05	1·08	1·14	1·20
3rd month	1·00	1·02	1·05	1·08	1·14	1·20
4th month	1·00	1·03	1·06	1·10	1·15	1·21
5th month	1·00	1·03	1·06	1·10	1·15	1·21
6th month	1·00	1·03	1·06	1·10	1·16	1·22
7th month	1·00	1·03	1·06	1·10	1·16	1·22
8th month	1·00	1·04	1·07	1·11	1·17	1·23
9th month	1·00	1·04	1·07	1·11	1·17	1·23
10th month	1·00	1·04	1·07	1·12	1·18	1·24
11th month	1·00	1·04	1·07	1·12	1·18	1·24
12th month	1·02	1·05	1·08	1·13	1·19	1·25

Fig. 7

Exercises 4G

1. How much is a £1 (special) certificate worth after:

a. 9 months, *b.* 1 year 7 months, *c.* 2 years 4 months, *d.* 3 years 3 months, *e.* 5 years 2 months, *f.* 6 years?

2. How much are: *a.* £300, *b.* £550, *c.* £125 worth of special issue savings certificates worth after:

   i. 2 years 7 months,

   ii. 4 years 7 months,

   iii. 5 years 7 months?

National Development Bonds and British Savings Bonds

These can be bought at most post offices and banks, including savings banks and through stockbrokers. They are sold in amounts of £5 and multiples of £5 and an investor may hold up to £2500 worth. Repayment on maturity is at the rate of £102 for £100 worth of bonds on the interest date next following 5 years after the date of purchase or in the case of bonds bought on an interest date, the fifth anniversary of purchase. Interest is at the rate of £5 per cent per annum and is payable half-yearly on 15th March and 15th September. A new issue of bonds with interest at $5\frac{1}{2}$ per cent per annum was made on 11th July 1966, and on 28th April 1969 they were replaced by 7% British Savings Bonds (First Issue).

Exercises 4H

1. Answer each of the following questions in each case giving a reason for your answer.

Can you buy *a.* £15, *b.* £28, *c.* £150, *d.* £1000, *e.* £2466, *f.* £3000 worth of national development bonds?

2. If a man purchased £500 worth of national development bonds on 15th March 1966, to how much total interest is he entitled

a. by 15th September 1966,   *b.* by 15th March 1967,

c. by 15th September 1969,   *d.* by 15th March 1971?

3. A man purchases the maximum possible number of national development bonds on 15th March 1966. How much are they worth if he withdraws them when they have reached their full mature value? What is the date when this happens? How much interest has he received during this period?

Summary

This chapter has dealt only with some of the more commonly used and useful services rendered to the community by the Post Office.

Many of the 'inland' services are available for overseas business, e.g. post, telephones, etc.

However, there are branches of post-office work which you could study individually. Some of these are listed below:

a. *Sale of licences.* Make a list of all the licences which are obtainable from the post office. Write down their cost, colour and the period of time for which they are issued, e.g. wireless, television, dog and motor-vehicle licences.

b. *Sale of stamps other than postage stamps.* Inquire at the post office about the sale of national insurance and national savings stamps. Make a list of the values available at present. Draw copies of these stamps in your book and label them with their value and colour.

c. *Payment of pensions and allowances.* Other than the allowances described earlier in the book, find out about *old age pensions* and *children's allowances*. Record the weekly amounts of each in your book, leaving space for changes.

For more detailed information about these services and also about the many overseas and other services rendered by the Post Office, you should study the *Post Office Guide,* on sale at most large post offices.

5 Insurance

What is insurance?

Insurance is a pooling and spreading of risks. For example, in a particular road there may be one fire in a year. If that householder were not insured, he could lose property and goods valued £2500. However, if he and a number of other householders each paid a sum into a general fund to be used in the case of fire, when such an accident did occur he would lose less financially or possibly not at all. Such a group action to offset great loss, through some unforeseeable accident, in the future, is called insuring against a particular risk.

The most common accidents that befall us all are:

i. death or injury,

ii. loss of house and/or furniture through fire, or other hazard, such as storm or tempest,

iii. loss of property.

People do not club together to produce a pool of money from which they draw after one of the above has occurred. Instead, today, there are companies and societies whose function it is to provide the householder, motorist and shopkeeper with an insurance to suit his needs. In fact, nowadays you can insure against almost anything—even against it raining on your holidays.

Life assurance

Many people who earn their living have others who are dependent upon them. Hence the one who earns is often called the 'breadwinner', and he (sometimes she) may be concerned for the future of his dependants in the event of his death or disablement through some accident. Therefore he approaches an insurance or assurance company and takes out a life assurance and in so doing agrees to pay the company a fixed sum each year, called a premium, until age 70 or death, whichever is the earlier. In return the company agrees to pay a fixed sum, say £1000, to his dependants if he dies during that period of years. Sometimes a lesser sum is paid to the man himself if he is seriously injured or disabled.

The amount of a life-assurance premium depends on the following factors.

i. The man's age next birthday—naturally the younger the man the smaller the risk of premature death and consequently the lower the premium.

ii. The amount of money he wishes his dependants to receive—the larger the amount the higher the annual premium.

Different companies charge different amounts, but the table below shows a representative selection of annual premiums for an amount of £100.

Table A

Age next birthday	£	Age next birthday	£	Age next birthday	£
21	1·55	28	1·70	35	2·00
22	1·56	29	1·73½	36	2·07½
23	1·58	30	1·77	37	2·15
24	1·60	31	1·81	38	2·25
25	1·62½	32	1·85	39	2·37½
26	1·65	33	1·90	40	2·52
27	1·67½	34	1·95	41	2·70

The following examples are based on this table:

Example 1

A young man aged 24 on his next birthday wishes to take out a life-assurance policy such that his relatives would receive £100 in the event of his premature death. What would be the annual premium?

From the table the premium per £100 at age 24 next birthday is £1·60. This is his annual premium.

Example 2

What would be the annual premiums if he wished his dependants to receive *a.* £500, *b.* £1 000? In each case calculate the quarterly payment.

Solution

a. For an assured sum of £500 he would have an annual premium of $5 \times £1·60 = £8$.

This equals $£\dfrac{8}{4} = £2$ per quarter.

b. For an assured sum of £1000 he would have an annual premium of $10 \times £1·60 = £16$.

This equals $£\dfrac{16}{4} = £4$ per quarter.

Exercises 5A

1. Use Table A.

What annual premium will be paid in each of the following cases:

a. a man aged 27 next birthday wishing to insure his life for £100,

b. a man aged 36 next birthday wishing to insure his life for £600,

c. a man aged 41 next birthday wishing to insure his life for £750,

d. a man aged 21 next birthday wishing to insure his life for £1 000,

e. a man aged 39 next birthday wishing to insure his life for £1 000?

2. A man aged 34 does not wish to spend more than £1 per month on life assurance. What is the maximum amount for which he can insure his life?

3. Explain why the amount in Table A increases as the age of the insured increases.

4. An insurance company pays 20 per cent of the premium to the agent who collects it.
Calculate:

a. the agent's share,

b. the net amount received by the company in Question 1.

5. The average expectation of life for a man today is 76 years. If each man in Question 1 dies at the age of 76 having paid his premium for that year, calculate:

a. for how many years he has to pay premiums before his death, *b*. the amount paid in premiums,

c. the amount received by the company.

How does the company make a profit?

Endowment assurance

Many people prefer this type of assurance, for although the premiums are higher it provides the same cover against a premature death as does a life-assurance policy, but has a term set on the number of years for which the premium shall be paid.

Assurance companies offer a wide choice of policies payable for anything up to 30 years, but generally they stipulate that the last premium must be paid before the insured's 70th birthday (some companies only assure up to age 65).

Once again the size of the premium depends on certain factors. These are:

1. The age of the insured on his (her) next birthday—the younger the insured the smaller the premium.
2. The amount of money which the insured wishes to be paid to his dependants or himself—the larger the sum the higher the premium.
3. The number of payments he wishes to make in one year—it costs more to pay a premium monthly than annually.
4. The number of years for which he intends to pay premiums—the longer the period the smaller the premium.

Before setting out tables of premiums, here is an example of an endowment-assurance policy.

A man may wish to assure his life for £1000. He is 40 next birthday and the longest period for which he can obtain a policy is 25 years. Throughout that period of 25 years, as long as he continues to pay his premiums regularly, his life is assured for £1000 and in the event of his premature death, the assurance company would pay his relatives £1000. If, however, he outlived the 25-year period the company would pay him the £1000.

Profits and bonuses

Assurance and insurance companies offer their policies with or without profits or bonuses.

For instance, a £1000 life-assurance policy may earn profits of about £30 per year, but generally they are not paid by the company until the policy is fully paid up.

The premiums for policies with profits are greater than those for policies without profits.

Here is an extract from an endowment life assurance with profits table— the sum assured is £500—the period is 20 years.

Table B

Age next birthday	Yearly £	Half yearly £	Quarterly £
20	25·40	13·15	6·60
21	25·45	13·20	6·65
22	25·55	13·25	6·70
23	25·65	13·30	6·75
24	25·75	13·35	6·80
25	26·00	13·40	6·85
26	26·25	13·45	6·90
27	26·50	13·50	6·95

Exercises 5B (Use Table B)

1. A man aged 23 next birthday wishes to invest in an endowment life assurance for £500 over 20 years. How much will it cost him per year and per quarter?

2. A man aged 22 wishes to invest $\frac{1}{12}$ of his net annual income of £1296 in endowment life assurance. What sum would be assured if he paid his premiums quarterly? If he decided to pay these premiums annually

a. how much would he save each year?

b. by how many complete £100 could he increase his sum assured for his original outlay?

3. Copy out and fill in the blanks in the following table:

Age next birthday	Sum assured	Yearly premium	Quarterly premium
27	£1000		
20		£5·08	
22			£1·34
		£20·60	
25	£2000		
23		Not to exceed £42	
21	£2500		

4. In each case in Question 3 how much would be saved by paying the premiums half-yearly instead of quarterly?

Motor car insurance

Insurance companies usually offer four tables of premiums for car insurances, two for comprehensive policies (these cover all risks) and two for third party cover only. It is an offence for a vehicle (car, motor-cycle, van, etc.) to be on the road without *third party insurance*. This is the insurance you take out to cover yourself against claims made by other people on you, should you be involved in any form of accident or incident. One comprehensive policy table and one third party policy table cover cars first registered before 1947 and consequently the engine size is described in Treasury (RAC) horsepower.

The other two tables are for cars registered in or after 1947, and the cubic capacity of the engine is the governing feature. Below are shown examples of:

(1) a pre-1947 third party policy table, and

(2) a post-1947 comprehensive policy table.

1. Pre-1947 third party policy

Treasury (RAC) h.p. not exceeding	District A	District B	District C	District D	District E
	£	£	£	£	£
9	7	8	9	10	12
12	8	9	11	12	14
15	9	10	12·50	14·50	16
17	10	11	14	16	18
20	11	12	15·50	18	20
23	12	13·50	17	19·50	22
26	13	14·50	18·50	21	23
30	14	16	20	22·50	25
35	15	17	21·50	24	27
41	16	18	23	25·50	29
Over 41	17	19	24	27	30

For fire and theft as well as third party add 75p per £100 or part thereof.

Capacity (cm^3) not exceeding	District A	District B	District C	District D	District E
	£	£	£	£	£
1100	18	22	26	32	38
1300	20	25	29	34	41
1600	23	28	32	39	47
2300	28	32	37	47	56
3000	33	38	45	55	65
3700	38	45	52	64	75
4500	47	54	63	77	87
Over 4500	54	63	74	89	99

For values exceeding £400, add £1 for each £200 or part of £200 over the initial £400.

Reductions in premium

Companies offer reductions in the premium whenever they consider that the risk of a claim is being made less. For instance, if only one driver drives the car, there is often a reduction of premium. If the owner offers to pay a percentage of each claim, the companies know this reduces the number of claims and increases the care taken by the drivers; consequently they will reduce the premium. Finally if an owner uses his vehicle and makes no claims upon the company, then his premiums are reduced each year up to a specific maximum reduction.

Car driven only by one named driver   10 per cent reduction
Policy holder agrees to pay first part of each
    accidental damage claim other than by fire
    or theft.

First £5	7$\frac{1}{2}$ per cent reduction
First £10	10 per cent reduction
First £20	15 per cent reduction

No claim discount:
    If there has been no claim on the policy for a period preceding renewal, the premium will be reduced as follows:

Period without a claim	Amount of reduction
One year	15 per cent
Two consecutive years	20 per cent
Three consecutive years	30 per cent
Four consecutive years	40 per cent

The insurance companies divide the country into *rating districts* (these are given at the end of this section) to which they give certain letters A—E, and this, too, affects the initial premium.

The policies, premiums, districts, rates and discounts vary from company to company. The tables and information quoted here are just an indication of some of the facts which must be considered before insuring a private car. Other information which refers to motor-cycle insurance is given later.

Example

A man living in Swindon (Wiltshire) owns a car of 2998 cm^3. He values the car at £1100.

  a. What would be the first, second and third annual premiums for a fully comprehensive policy if no claim is made on the company?

  b. What would be the effect on the first premium if the owner stated:

   i. he would only drive the car himself, and

   ii. he would also pay the first £20 of each claim?

Solution

  a. District: Swindon (Wiltshire) = A.

   £1100 = £400 + £700 (the £700 makes four lots of £200 or part thereof at £1 per £200).

   £

   Premium £33 + £4 = 37·00 in the first year.
   15 per cent reduction is 5·55
   _____

   ∴ Net premium is   31·45 in the second year.
   20 per cent (of £37) is 7·40
   _____

   ∴ Net premium is   29·60 in the third year.

  b. (*i*) £37 premium in the first year; 10 per cent reduction for one driver is £3·70. This leaves £33·30.

   (*ii*) 15 per cent (of £33·30) reduction for paying the first £20 of any claim is £4·98$\frac{1}{2}$.

    ∴ Net premium is £28·31$\frac{1}{2}$.

Rating districts

ABERDEENSHIRE	A	AYRSHIRE	A
ANGLESEY	A	BANFFSHIRE	A
ANGUS	A	BEDFORDSHIRE	C
ARGYLLSHIRE	A	BERKSHIRE	B

BERWICKSHIRE	A	LEICESTERSHIRE	C
BRECKNOCKSHIRE	A	LINCOLNSHIRE	B
BUCKINGHAMSHIRE	C	LONDON	
CAERNARVONSHIRE	A	(*i*) London Postal Area	E
CAITHNESS	A	(*ii*) Metropolitan Police Area	
CAMBRIDGESHIRE	B	excluding (*i*)	D
CARDIGANSHIRE	A	MIDDLESEX*	C
CARMARTHENSHIRE	A	MIDLOTHIAN	C
CHESHIRE	C	MONMOUTHSHIRE	A
CLACKMANNANSHIRE	A	MORAY	A
CORNWALL	A	NAIRNSHIRE	A
CUMBERLAND	B	NORFOLK	B
DENBIGHSHIRE	B	NORTHAMPTONSHIRE	C
DERBYSHIRE	C	NORTHUMBERLAND	C
DEVON	A	NOTTINGHAMSHIRE	C
DORSET	A	OXFORDSHIRE	B
DUNBARTONSHIRE*	A	PEEBLES-SHIRE	A
DUMFRIESSHIRE	A	PEMBROKESHIRE	A
DURHAM (COUNTY)	C	PERTHSHIRE	A
EASTLOTHIAN	A	RADNORSHIRE	A
ESSEX*	C	RENFREWSHIRE*	C
FIFE	A	ROSS and CROMARTY	A
FLINTSHIRE	B	ROXBURGHSHIRE	A
GLAMORGANSHIRE	C	RUTLANDSHIRE	C
GLASGOW CITY		SELKIRKSHIRE	A
and surrounding areas	E	SHROPSHIRE	B
GLOUCESTERSHIRE	A	SOMERSET	A
HAMPSHIRE	B	STAFFORDSHIRE	C
HEREFORDSHIRE	A	STIRLINGSHIRE	A
HERTFORDSHIRE*	C	SUFFOLK	B
HUNTINGDONSHIRE	C	SURREY*	C
INVERNESS-SHIRE	A	SUSSEX	B
KENT*	C	SUTHERLAND	A
KINCARDINESHIRE	A	WARWICKSHIRE	C
KINROSS-SHIRE	A	WESTLOTHIAN	C
KIRCUDBRIGHTSHIRE	A	WESTMORLAND	B
LANARKSHIRE*	C	WIGTOWNSHIRE	A
LANCASHIRE		WILTSHIRE	A
(*i*) South of the River Ribble	D	WORCESTERSHIRE	B
(*ii*) North of Morecambe Bay		YORKSHIRE	C
and West of River Kent	B		
(*iii*) North of River Ribble			
excluding (*ii*)	C		

* Excluding those parts of these counties which are within the London or Glasgow areas.

Exercises 5C

Now work the following examples—find the premium in the first year for a comprehensive policy (for those cars registered after 1947) and a third party policy (a) with and (b) without fire and theft cover (for those cars registered before 1947).

District	Size of car engine	Value £	Special condition
1. Leeds	1700 cm^3	840	
2. Manchester	1008 cm^3	520	
3. Hereford	884 cm^3	585	
4. Central London	1260 cm^3	1000	First £5 of each claim
5. Brighton	3280 cm^3	1850	First £10 of each claim, one driver only
6. Exeter	14 h.p.	320	
7. Holyhead	1285 cm^3	740	
8. Cambridge	2142 cm^3	1780	One driver
9. Blackpool	24 h.p.	410	First £20 of each claim
10. Nottingham	1590 cm^3	785	No claims for 3 years already
11. Glasgow	11·8 h.p.	250	
12. Luton	1147 cm^3	800	No claims for 2 years
13. Aylesbury	848 cm^3	375	
14. Llandudno	1500 cm^3	1850	No claims for 10 years
15. Peterborough	18 h.p.	250	One named driver
16. Cambridge	1800 cm^3	800	
17. Birkenhead	16 h.p.	395	
18. Stirling	21·6 h.p.	520	First £10 of each claim
19. Ayr	3702 cm^3	2300	No claim for 4 years
20. Colchester	7·8 h.p.	50	
21. Southampton	2498 cm^3	1875	
22. Tenby	3202 cm^3	1400	
23. Cardiff	1347 cm^3	1250	
24. John o' Groats	32 h.p.	410	First £20 of each claim

Motor cycle insurance

The premiums are set out in the next three tables for: (a) third party, (b) third party, fire and theft, and (c) comprehensive policies.

The cover given by the insurance companies is specifically limited:

in (a) to cover claims *against* the insured from accidents connected with using the motor-cycle;

in (b) to cover all in (a) and also loss or damage to cycle due to fire or theft;

in (c) all in (b) and also any accidental damage.

No-claims discounts are similar to those for car policy holders, namely:

Period of insurance	Reduction
The preceding year	10 per cent
The preceding 2 consecutive years	15 per cent
The preceding 3 consecutive years	20 per cent
The preceding 4 consecutive years	25 per cent

Additional insurances are available as follows:

i. Personal accident benefits from £0·50 to £1·50 per person.

ii. Third party indemnity to cover death of sidecar passenger(s) at £0·50 per seat.

iii. Additional drivers—add 25 per cent.

Table 1. Third party

Cubic capacity not exceeding	District A	District B	District C	District D	District E
cm³	£	£	£	£	£
50	0·75	1·00	1·00	1·25	1·25
100	1·00	1·25	1·25	1·50	1·75
200	2·50	2·50	2·50	3·00	3·25
350	3·50	3·75	4·00	5·00	5·25
500	4·25	4·75	5·25	6·00	6·75
Over 500	4·75	5·75	6·75	7·75	8·50

Table 2. Third party, fire and theft

Cubic capacity not exceeding	District A	District B	District C	District D	District E
cm³	£	£	£	£	£
50	1·00	1·25	1·25	1·50	1.50
100	1·50	1·75	1·75	2·00	2·25
200	3·00	3·00	3·00	4·00	4·25
350	4·50	4·75	5·00	6·00	6·25
500	5·25	5·75	6·25	7·50	8·50
Over 500	5·75	6·75	7·75	9·00	10·50

Table 3. Comprehensive

Cubic capacity not exceeding	District A	District B	District C	District D	District E
cm³	£	£	£	£	£
50	2·00	2·25	2·25	2·50	2·50
100	3·50	3·75	3·75	4·00	4·25
200	7·00	7·50	8·00	9·50	10·50
350	13·00	13·50	14·00	16·00	18·00
500	20·00	23·00	25·00	27·00	31·00
Over 500	23·00	25·00	27·00	31·00	34·00

Additional premiums

Additional premiums are required from persons who have held a driving licence for less than a year as follows:

Size of engine	Tables 1 and 2	Table 3
	£	£
Not exceeding 50 cm³	0·25	0·50
Not exceeding 100 cm³	0·50	0·75
Not exceeding 200 cm³	0·75	1·50
Not exceeding 350 cm³	1·25	2·50
Not exceeding 500 cm³	2·00	4·00
exceeding 500 cm³	2·50	5·00

Drivers aged 16–18 years are restricted to insuring cycles of less than 250 cm³ and the total premiums are increased by 75 per cent.

For drivers aged 18–25 years, the total premiums are increased by 25 per cent.

Example

Find the cost to

a. an 18-year-old boy who has been driving for over 2 years,

b. a 27-year-old man who has been driving for less than 1 year,

of comprehensively insuring a motor-cycle of 242 cm³ capacity; rating district C.

Solution

Comprehensive insurance, Table 3.

a. Cubic capacity 200–350 cm³, district C, basic premium £14·00, add to this 16–18 increase of 75 per cent = £14 + £10·50 = £24·50.

b. Cubic capacity 242 cm³, district C, basic premium £14, add to this first-year driver's extra £2·50 = £16·50.

Exercises 5D

1. Calculate the cost to a 21-year-old who has been driving for 2 years of third party insurance if he owns a 347 cm³ motor-cycle and the cycle is garaged:

a. in Exeter (Devon),

b. in Maidstone (Kent),

c. in Worcester.

2. Repeat Question 1:

i. for third party, fire and theft insurance;

ii. for a comprehensive policy.

3. A 28-year-old motor cyclist who has been driving for 10 years decides to insure his 498 cm³ motor-cycle; he lives in Liverpool. Find the cost of each type of premium. He has no no-claim discount (or bonus).

4. A 16-year-old buys and wishes to insure a 125 cm³ motor-cycle. Find the cost of comprehensive insurance if he lives

a. in Brighton, Sussex,

b. in Stratford, Warwickshire.

5. Copy out and fill in the blanks in the following table:

Age of driver	Years of driving exp.	Size of eng.	District	Rating District A–E	Third party prem.	Third party F. and T. prem.	Comp. prem.	Comp. prem. with max. no-claim discount in £
a. 40	10	134	Oxford					
b. 17	1	396	Leeds					
c. 16	0	122	Edinburgh					
d. 22	4	251	Bath					
e. 35	7	510	Ipswich					
f. 23	3	148	Derby					
g. 27	0	264	Southport					

Other insurance policies

Most householders will insure both their house and their furniture against fire and other hazards.

Common rates of insurance are shown below:

	Comprehensive	Fire only
House	10p per £100 (25p for fully comprehensive with no exclusions)	7½p per £100
Furniture	20p per £100	5p to 10p per £100

Individual items like cameras can be insured at £1·25 per £100.

Exercises 5E

1. Find the premiums to be paid for a comprehensive (10p per £100) insurance on a house valued £4500 and a comprehensive insurance on the contents valued at £800 (20p per £100).

2. What would be the cost of:

a. fire insurance only (7½p per £100),

b. a comprehensive insurance (10p per £100) on the following properties:

  i. a house valued £5000,

  ii. a house valued £2000,

  iii. a farm costing £10000,

  iv. a factory costing £100000?

3. What would be the cost of insuring furniture valued at

a. £200, *b.* £650, *c.* £1200, at:

  i. 20p per £100,

  ii. 6p per £100?

4. What would be the cost of insuring the following:

a. cine camera value £120,   *b.* tape recorder value £80,

c. stamp collection value £550,   *d.* gold watch value £330,

e. binoculars and telescope value £40 and £72 respectively?

6 Buying a house

Many people need to borrow some money when they wish to purchase a house. There are four different sources from which they can obtain a loan. They are:

i. a building society,
ii. a bank,
iii. a borough or county council,
iv. a private individual.

The building society will require a deposit—probably between one-tenth and one-fifth of the value of the house—and will lend the balance if they consider the house is worth this amount and if they are reasonably certain the borrower can repay the loan with interest in a specified time. Borrowing money to pay for a house is called *raising a mortgage*.

The rate of interest charged has varied recently between 6 and 9 per cent per annum.

Methods of calculating mortgage repayments
Method A
Most building societies charge a fixed amount per month, quarter, etc., which covers both loan repayment and mortgage interest. The actual calculations for the first few years of repayment of a loan of £1440 over 8 years at 6 per cent are shown on page 70:

Cost price of house   £1600—purchased April 1966
Deposit (10 per cent) £160

Sum borrowed   £1440
Interest   6 per cent per annum (on amount owing)
Repayment   £240 per annum (£20 per month)

		£	*Interest at 6 per cent* £	£
Amount owing in April 1966		1440		
Amount paid off loan		153·6* +	86·4† =	240
Amount owing in April 1967		1286·4		
Amount paid off loan		162·816 +	77·184 =	240
Amount owing in April 1968		1123·584		
Amount paid off loan		172·585 +	67·4150 =	240
	1969	950·999		
		182·9401 +	57·0599 =	240
	1970	768·0589		
		193·9164 +	46·0836 =	240
	1971	574·1425		
		205·5515 +	34·4485 =	240
	1972	368·5910		
		217·8845 +	22·1155 =	240
	1973	150·7065		

This will take eight monthly payments at least, seven of £20 each and one of the balance of the debt plus the interest due on the debt for this period of 8 months.

$$£150\cdot7065 \times \frac{6}{100} \times \frac{\overset{4}{\cancel{8}}}{\underset{\cancel{2}}{12}} = £6\cdot02826$$

Total = £156·73476
∴ 7 payments of £20 and 1 of £16·74.

* £240 − 6 per cent of £1440 = £153·6.
† 6 per cent of £1440 = £86·4.

The following calculation is similar to the one just worked, but in all cases the amounts are kept to complete pounds.

Cost price of house   £1600—purchased April 1966
Deposit (10 per cent)   160
                         ————
Sum borrowed   1440
Interest 6 per cent per annum
Repayment   £240 per annum (£20 per month)
Amount owing April 1966 £1440.

Interest at 6 per cent on amount owing $\dfrac{1440 \times 6}{100} = £86\cdot4$.

The building society will regard this interest as £87.

		Interest			
	£	£		£	
Amount paid off loan	153	+ 87	=	240	
Amount owing in April 1967	1287				
Amount paid off loan	162	+ 78	=	240	
	————				
Amount owing in April 1968	1125				
	172	+ 68	=	240	
	————				
1969	953				
	182	+ 58	=	240	
	————				
1970	771				
	193	+ 47	=	240	
	————				
1971	578				
	205	+ 35	=	240	
	————				
1972	373				
	217	+ 23	=	240	
	————				
	156				

Interest on £156 at 6 per cent for 9 months = £7
£156 + £7 = £163 = 8 payments of £20 + 1 of £3.

Note. The paper-work is greatly simplified and the difference to the borrower is £6·26 over the course of 8 years.

During your calculations, remember that if you are working to the next whole £ you can correct your figure to be multiplied so as to ignore units of £.

i.e. £1287 becomes £1290, £1290 × $\dfrac{6}{100}$ = £77·4 and this is taken as £78.

Exercises 6A

Work the following examples using the *simplified* method which has just been outlined. (Note the interest for each year is calculated at the start of each year.)

1. A man buys a bungalow costing £2000 through a building society. His deposit is £200 and he repays £20 a month starting in January 1967. The interest rate is 6 per cent. How much did he owe in January 1970?

2. In April 1960 a man owed £400 on a house and was repaying at the rate of £7·50 per month with interest at 5 per cent.

   a. When will the loan be repaid?

   b. How much interest has the man paid altogether?

3. A man bought a house for £4000. He put down £1500 (i.e. deposit) and borrowed the rest from a building society at 4 per cent. After making four repayments of £300 per annum (£25 per month) the interest rate went up to $6\frac{1}{2}$ per cent. How much of the loan is still owing after he makes the fifth repayment?

4. A small agency for a building society showed the following loans:

Date April	Name	Type	Price paid	Deposit	Loan	Monthly repayment	Interest rate
1961	Mr J. Brown	House	£3800	£1300	£2500	£25	4 per cent
1962	Mrs O. Walker	Bungalow	£6000	£1000	£5000	£40	4 per cent
1963	Mr P. Cape	House	£2750	£300	£2450	£15	5 per cent
1964	Mr J. Riley	Shop premises	£1400	£140	£1260	£18	5 per cent
1965	Mr and Mrs Small	Flat	£750	£100	£650	£10	$6\frac{1}{2}$ per cent

How much is still owing on each loan after the repayment made in April 1967? Give all your answers to the nearest £. (Assume that the first payment for each year is made in May.)

5. If a man borrowed £3000 in 1960 and repaid £35 per month (£420 per annum) starting in January 1960 to cover interest and loan repayment and the interest was calculated at 4 per cent:

   a. Find out how long it would take to repay the debt.

   b. If in December 1963 interest rates were raised to 6 per cent to take effect from January 1964 onwards calculate:

   i. how much longer he would have to go on making repayments, and

   ii. how much more he would have to pay.

Legal and road charges

When buying a house or land there are certain formalities that must be gone through to ensure that firstly the seller is legally entitled to sell the house or land and secondly that the purchaser will become the legal owner when the sale is completed.

It is quite essential that the purchaser employs a solicitor to negotiate transfers of this nature, as there must be an agreement in writing between the parties, the subject of the sale must be clearly described and located, the right of seller to sell must be investigated and established and the purchaser must receive from the seller 'deeds' which establish legal ownership. For all this a solicitor is entitled to make a charge which is often determined by the purchase price of the land or house for sale. There are sometimes other initial charges which can be encountered when purchasing a house, such as road charges. This is an amount specified by the local authority per foot of frontage of the land on which the house stands and it covers the cost of laying pavement, building roads and installing the main services.

Exercises 6B
In the following cases find the total cost of the houses:

1. *Address*	*Purchase Price*	*Legal charges*	*Road charges*
	£	£	£
8 Dover Road	2450	40·00	74·34
16 Walmer Road	1950	30·50	92·08
35 Park Avenue	4850	85·75	44·00
73 Leamington Road	2985	43·50	132·60
17 Crosby Road	3400	56·00	108·40

2. Calculate the amount of money required in Question 1 to complete each purchase if the buyer borrows not more than 85 per cent of the purchase price and finds the rest himself.*

3. George Brown had £1600 in the bank when he decided to buy 8 Abercrombie Square. The purchase price of this house was £4360 and he paid £450 to the estate agents as a deposit. The building society offered to advance £3270 on mortgage. Legal and other necessary fees came to a total of £248·60 and the costs of removal of furniture were £74.

a. What percentage of the purchase price was the building society willing to pay?

---

* Building Societies stipulate that they will lend not more than a specific percentage (say 85 per cent) of the purchase price and this is rounded off downwards to the nearest multiple of £25.

E.g. in Ex. 6B. No. 2, 85 per cent of £2450 = £2082·50, Building Society would lend £2075 (possibly in some cases £2100—but this would exceed 85 per cent).

b. What was the total cost of the house including fees, but *not* including removal costs?

c. How much had George Brown in the bank when all bills were settled?

Method B

Most building societies charge a fixed amount per year, quarter, month or week, and the amount of this charge is calculated using a ready-made scale of charges.

Example 1

John Gregson wishes to buy a house costing £3250 and needs to borrow money. One building society offers to lend him 80 per cent of the purchase price on mortgage, but specifies that the monthly repayments must not be greater than 20 per cent of his gross income, which is £1260 per annum. The building society also surveys the property prior to offering the mortgage and charges £5·25 for this service. Legal and other charges amount to £88.

Using Table A on page 75:

a. Calculate how much the building society is offering to advance,

b. What is the monthly repayment on this loan:

    i. over 10 years,

    ii. over 15 years,

    iii. over 20 years,

    iv. over 25 years?

c. Calculate how much Mr Gregson will have to find in order to complete the purchase.

d. What is the minimum period of time over which Mr Gregson can make repayments, taking notice of the conditions imposed by the building society?

Solution

a. Building society advance 80 per cent of £3250 $= \dfrac{80 \times 3250}{100} = £2600.$

b. Years:	10	15	20	25
£2500	29·50	23·00	19·50	17·50
£100	1·18	0·92	0·78	0·70
Monthly repayment:	30·68	23·92	20·28	18·20

$$£$$

c. Mr Gregson must find £3 250 − £2 600 = 650·00

+ survey fees   5·25

+ legal and other charges   88·00

                        Total £743·25

d. Salary = £1 260 per annum = £105 per month.

20 per cent of £105 = £21 per month.

Repayments must not exceed £21 per month on £2 600.

The minimum period for the loan must therefore be 20 years (£21 per month lies between £23·92—15 years, and £20·28—20 years, and as the repayments must not exceed £21 per month the period of repayment is 20 years).

Example 2

If Mr Gregson wishes to set aside a sum from his income weekly in order to cover his mortgage repayments, how much will this sum be?

Solution

The 20-year repayment scale is £20·28 per month.

12 × £20·28 = £243·36 per annum.

Total annual repayment is £243·36.

Weekly repayment is $\dfrac{£243·36}{52}$ = £4·68.

Table A

Loan	Calendar monthly payments			
	10-year term	15-year term	20-year term	25-year term
£	£	£	£	£
100	1·18	0·92	0·78	0·70
250	2·95	2·30	1·95	1·75
500	5·90	4·60	3·90	3·50
750	8·85	6·90	5·85	5·25
1 000	11·80	9·20	7·80	7·00
1 250	14·75	11·50	9·75	8·75
1 500	17·70	13·80	11·70	10·50
1 750	20·65	16·10	13·65	12·25
2 000	23·60	18·40	15·60	14·00
2 250	26·55	20·70	17·55	15·75
2 500	29·50	23·00	19·50	17·50

Exercises 6C

Using the scale of charges shown in Table A, work the following examples:

1. Mr Jackson buys a bungalow and obtains a mortgage of £1 400. How much (*a*) per calendar month, and (*b*) per week, will the repayments be if he agrees to repay over (*i*) 10 years, (*ii*) 15 years, (*iii*) 25 years?

2. A building society offers to lend Mr Wainwright 90 per cent of the cost of a house, advertised at £2 750. If all other expenses amount to £81·50, how much will Mr Wainwright have to find to complete the purchase?

3. Henry Wilson wishes to purchase a shop, flat and garage advertised at £5000 and asks a building society for a mortgage. They offer him 85 per cent of the purchase price. He agrees to repay the money over 15 years. His legal and other fees amount to £248·20, removal expenses £71·50, and other expenses, shop fitting, etc. £286·35.

   a. How much does he borrow from the building society?

   b. How much money has he to find to complete the purchase?

   c. If prior to this transaction his bank account stood at £1 762·40, how much will he have in the bank when all his bills are settled?

   d. As he is repaying over 15 years

      i. what is the annual repayment for £100 borrowed,

      ii. what is the total annual repayment on the mortgage advanced to him,

      iii. what sum must be set aside each week to cover his mortgage repayments.

   e. If during the first year of business in this shop his gross profits amounted to £34 per week, what percentage of his gross profits is he using to make his mortgage repayment?

4. A man wishes to buy a shop and flat valued at £5000 and inquires from various building societies about a mortgage. He has already received an estimate of all the other costs involved in moving and setting up in a new business. These other costs are legal charges £145; removal expenses £75; purchase of stock £1 200 and shop fittings £215. If his bank balance is £2885, what is the minimum mortgage, both in £ and as a percentage that will meet his needs? If he repays his mortgage over 10 years, what will be his monthly repayment? What percentage are his annual repayments of his net income of £3000 per annum?

7 Owner or tenant

Rates

All house-owners and also some people who pay rent have to pay rates to their local council for the services which that council provides. These services are listed on the back of a rate demand note and include the provision of schools, libraries, houses and roads and paying the salaries or wages of policemen, teachers and local government employees.

House and landowners pay a sum which is calculated by the Rating or Valuation Officer's department and depends on the area of land and in the case of houses the size and number of rooms and the amenities attached to or built in the house, such as garages and other outbuildings, central heating installations, etc.

This figure is called the rateable value (R.V.) of the property and the sum of the rateable values of all the land and properties in a county borough or county area is termed the total rateable value of the property in the borough (or county).

The Borough Treasurer's department prepares an estimate of the total cost of providing all the services required by various committees of the council. Taking into account government grants and any other income, the council's estimated expenditure and any other expenses such as loan debts, the amount to be raised by the rates is then calculated.

Example

A County Borough has a total rateable value of £600000. How much would be raised by:

  a. a rate of £1 in the £,
  b. a rate of 50p in the £,
  c. a rate of 55p in the £,
  d. a rate of 1p in the £?

Solution

  a. $£600\,000 \times \dfrac{£1}{£1} = £600\,000,$

  b. $£600\,000 \times \dfrac{50p}{£1} = £600\,000 \times \dfrac{1}{2} = £300\,000,$

  c. $£600\,000 \times \dfrac{55p}{£1} = £600\,000 \times \dfrac{55}{100} = £330\,000,$

  d. $£600\,000 \times \dfrac{1p}{£1} = £600\,000 \times \dfrac{1}{100} = £6\,000$

The figure £6000 in this example is called the product, or produce, or yield of a 1p rate and is obtained by dividing the total rateable value by 100.

If this figure is known, it is fairly easy to calculate the rate required to balance a borough's account.

For instance, in the case of the above borough:

$$\begin{array}{rr} & £ \\ \text{If the council's estimates} = & 396\,520 \\ \text{Loan debt interest} = & 68\,656 \\ \hline \therefore \text{ total charges} = & 465\,176 \\ \text{Income from government grants etc.} = & 97\,500 \\ \hline \text{Amount to be raised by rates} = & 367\,676 \end{array}$$

$$\text{Rates} = \frac{367\,676}{6\,000} \text{ p in the £.}$$

$$\text{Rate} = 61 \cdot 279 \text{p in the £.}$$

The fraction must not be ignored, otherwise insufficient money would be raised, therefore the rates would be 62p in the £.

Example

A certain property may have a rateable value of £60, how much must the owner pay in rates?

Solution

The rate is 62p in the £.

The rates would be $60 \times 62p = £37 \cdot 20$.

Exercises 7A

1. Calculate the rates paid in the following cases.

Rateable value in £	Rate
	p
110	40
77	47
45	51
104	50
136	57
95	62

2. Complete the following table. The first line is worked for you.

Town	Total R.V. in £	Estimate of council in £	Rate
A	800 000	440 000	$£\frac{440}{800} = 55p$ in the £
B	1 200 000	720 000	
C	450 000	288 000	
D	700 000	367 500	
E	400 000		$42\frac{1}{2}p$
F		700 000	56p
G	1 240 000		55p
H		2 240 760	71p

The following statement shows how the rate in the pound is made up and is a summary of the reverse side of a rate demand. To calculate the total amount paid in rates multiply the rate by the rateable value.

	p
Education	41·52
Public health	8·95
Welfare	3·85
Housing	3·04
Police	9·45
Fire	2·25
Highways	7·03
Parks and gardens	3·08
Museum and library	1·40
Publicity and entertainment	2·08
Town planning	0·30
Other services, contingencies and improvements	7·05
	90·00

Total from previous page	90·00
Deduct housing and other government grants	41·86
	48·14
Add services administered by Committees	0·86
Rate in the £ payable by ratepayer	49p

The water rate is 7p in the £.

The estimated product of a new penny rate is £25 860.

Payment should be made in two equal instalments, one in April and the second in October.

Use this information to answer Questions 1–5 in Exercises 7B.

Exercises 7B

1. What rates would a householder pay if his house is assessed at £104? How much would be due at each instalment

    a. on the general rates,

    b. on water rates,

    c. for all rates?

2. Repeat Question 1 for properties of R.V.: *i.* £64, *ii.* £85, *iii.* £126, *iv.* £180.

3. What is the total rateable value of the town? What would be the income from the rates in 1968 if the rates were 49p in the £. If the rates increased to 52p in 1969, by how much would the income increase?

4. A householder living in this town pays £37·24 in general rates—what is the R.V. of his house?

5. Draw a pie chart to represent the amount required for each of the main services rendered by the council as shown in the estimate (page 79).

    (*Note.* If 90p is equivalent to 360° then 1p will be represented by 4°.)

6. A man sells a house of R.V. £54 in a town where the rates are 70p in the £. He buys another house where the rates are 63p in the £ and finds that his rates are just twice as much. What is the R.V. of the second house?

7. A town of rateable value £160 000 needs to raise £17 600 for a new swimming pool. By how much will the rates be increased?

8. A householder in the above town owned a house R.V. £88. If the general rates were 62p in the £ before the increase, what are his rates before and after the increase?

Renting a house

Rent is a sum of money charged by an owner of property to the occupier or tenant. The tenant (who pays the rent) has certain responsibilities, as does the landlord. If each carries out his part of the transaction honestly and thoughtfully, then both sides will be satisfied.

The rent charged should cover repairs to the fabric of the house and its major installations (but not usually decoration of the rooms, wallpaper, paint, distemper, etc.) It should cover renewals of worn-out parts, e.g. roofs and gutters, etc. (but not usually improvements to the existing facilities). The rent may include a contribution towards the rates or this can be paid completely either by the landlord or the tenant depending on the terms of the tenancy.

Exercises 7C

1. Find out the meaning of the following terms in connexion with rent payments:

a. rent collector, *b.* landlord, *c.* tenant, *d.* arrears, *e.* premises.

2. Below is shown a page from a rent book:

Date	Rent	Rates	Arrears	Total due	Total paid	Signature
	£	£	£	£	£	
14th July	2·60	0·95	—	3·55	3·55	H. Evans
21st July	2·60	0·95	—	3·55	3·55	H. Evans
28th July	2·60	0·95	—	3·55	—	—
4th August	2·60	0·95	3·55	7·10	—	—
11th August	2·60	0·95	7·10	10·65	10·65	H. Evans

a. What is the weekly rent?

b. How much is this per year?

c. What is the amount paid weekly in rates?

d. What is the annual amount paid in rates?

e. What is the total weekly sum due?

f. What is the total amount paid to the collector?

g. Who is the biggest landlord in most towns?

h. Why do you think this tenant was in arrears on the 4th and 11th August?

j. At what time in the year is the 'rates' part of the weekly payment likely to change and why?

k. For what reason is the 'rent' part of the payment likely to change?

l. Discuss the advantages and disadvantages of (*a*) owning (*b*) renting a house.

8 House and garden

This chapter will discuss the cost of maintaining and possibly improving the premises in which you live.

Wallpaper

This is sold in rolls which are usually about 11 metres long by 52 cm (0·52 m) wide. Today wallpaper is prepacked and ready trimmed, but until recently it was sold with a narrow border just over 1 cm wide which had to be removed before the paper was cut and pasted.

If you wish to buy wallpaper, the assistant will probably tell you how much paper you need from his own ready reckoner, but they often over-estimate and can sometimes cause unnecessary expense, particularly when the paper is expensive. So you should be able to estimate for your own satisfaction the number of rolls needed to paper a room.

A simple approximate method of calculating the number of rolls of wallpaper needed to paper a room is as follows:

  a. find the perimeter of the room (P metres),

  b. find the height of the room from the top of the skirting board (H metres),

  c. multiply P by H and divide by W (the width of the wallpaper to be used in metres),

  d. divide the result by 11 (the number of metres of paper in one roll).

The number that is left is the number of rolls of paper required to completely cover the walls of the room. Due allowance must be made for windows and doors. Finally, using an approximation of this sort, allow at least an extra half-roll above the final number calculated.

Example
A room is 6 metres by 4 metres and 2·6 metres from skirting board to ceiling.
   Find the number of rolls of wallpaper required to paper the walls of this room.

Solution
$P = 6\,m \times 2 + 4\,m \times 2 = 20\,m$
$H = 2\cdot6\,m$
$$\frac{P \times H}{11W} = \frac{20 \times 2\cdot6}{11 \times 0\cdot52} = \frac{100}{11} = 9\tfrac{1}{11} \text{ rolls}$$
$\therefore$ 10 rolls are required.

This is about the number of rolls required to paper all the walls of this room. As it must contain at least one door and probably two or more windows, 10 rolls would be quite adequate.
   Most shopkeepers will set aside a further roll or two from the same batch if you ask them to do so.

Exercises 8A
1. Make a sketch showing the four walls of a room 4 m by 3 m by 2·6 m high. On each long wall is a door 2·2 m high by 0·75 m wide and on one short wall is a window 2·6 m long by 1·1 m high. There is a skirting board 0·14 m high all round the room and the door frames are 0·03 m wide. Calculate the number of rolls of paper required to paper the room.
2. Calculate the number of rolls of wallpaper required to paper each of the rooms below:

	Length	Width	Height	Height of skirting board and door frame	Size and number of doors	Area of cupboards, windows, etc.
	m	m	m	m	m	m²
a.	4	3	2·5	0·07	2 × 0·7 (1)	3
b.	8	3·5	2·4	0·08	2 × 0·7 (1)	6
c.	6	4	3	0·10	2·2 × 0·8 (2)	5·5
d.	3·5	3·5	2·4	0·07	2 × 0·75 (2)	5
e.	4·1	3·2	2·3	0·065	2 × 0·7 (1)	2

3. The following diagrams are plan views of rooms. The doors shown thus ⌒ are all 2 m × 0·7 m. Fireplaces are labelled F and are 1 m high. The skirting board is made of timber 0·07 m × 0·02 m. The windows shown thus ⊣ ⊢ are all 1 m high. The rooms are 2·5 m high.

Calculate:

a. the area of the floor, and

b. the number of rolls of wallpaper required to paper the walls and the cost of the paper.

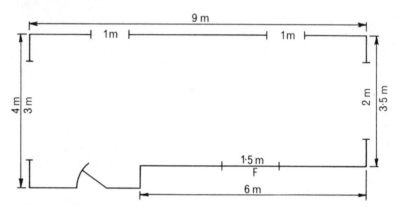

Fig. 7   i. paper at 44p per roll

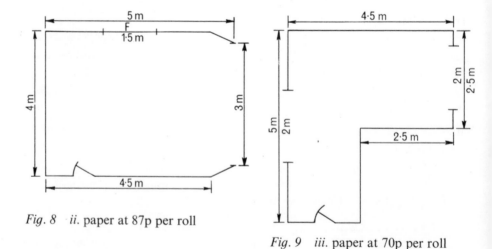

Fig. 8   ii. paper at 87p per roll

Fig. 9   iii. paper at 70p per roll

Papering the ceiling

Ceiling paper is sold in exactly the same lengths and widths as wallpaper, but in calculating the amount of paper required, care should be taken to make sure that there will be no joins on the ceiling. In the room mentioned in *Exercises 8A* Question 1 there are two ways of estimating and papering the ceiling.

Method A

Number of 3·5 m lengths required $= \dfrac{4 \text{ m}}{0·52 \text{ m}} = \dfrac{400}{52} = 7\tfrac{9}{13}$,

that is 8 lengths.

Number of 3·5 m lengths that can be cut from a 11 m roll $= 3$.

Number of rolls required $= \dfrac{8}{3} = 2\tfrac{2}{3}$ rolls, therefore 3 rolls must be bought.

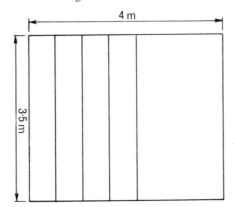

Fig. 10

Method B

Number of 4 m lengths required $= \dfrac{3·5 \text{ m}}{0·52 \text{ m}} = \dfrac{350}{52} = 6\tfrac{19}{26}$,

that is 7 lengths.

Number of 4 m lengths that can be cut from a 11 m roll $= 2$ (waste on each roll $= 3$ m).

Number of rolls required $= \dfrac{7}{2} = 3\tfrac{1}{2}$ rolls, therefore 4 rolls must be bought.

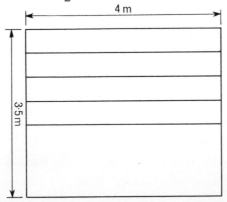

Fig. 11

It can be seen from the above calculations that method B is more expensive than method A. However, not all rooms are so simple in shape and the calculations are often a little more complicated.

Whilst discussing ceilings, a modern method of covering them is to use polystyrene tiles which come in a variety of sizes.

Common sizes of ceiling tile are: 0.25 m square (0.25 m $\times$ 0.25 m)

0.50 m square.

To calculate the number of 0.25 m square tiles required to cover a rectangular ceiling, multiply the length by the breadth of the room in metres, giving your answer to the next highest whole number and multiply this number by 16.

Example

Find the number of 0.25 m square tiles required to cover a ceiling 3 m by 4 m.

Solution

3 m $\times$ 4 m $= 12$ m^2.

$12 \times 16 = 192$ tiles.

This calculation may give slightly more than are actually necessary, for some of the part or cut tiles can be used again. However, it is not a big overestimate and many other methods would produce an underestimate.

Exercises 8B

1. Copy out the following table and fill in the blanks:

Size of room	Cost of ceiling paper per roll	No. of rolls req'd	Cost to paper ceiling	Cost of each 0·25 m tile	No. of tiles req'd	Cost of 0·25 m tiling	Cost of each 0·5 m tile	No. of tiles req'd	Cost of 0·5 m tiling
4m × 3m	45p			2p			8p		
3·5m × 4·5m	31p			2½p			12p		
4m square	52p			3p			16p		
7m × 3·5m	60p			5p			24p		

2. Find:

  i. the area of the ceiling (to the nearest m^2),

  ii. the number of rolls of paper required, and

  iii. the cost of papering the ceiling in paper costing 45p a roll for each of the rooms in *Exercises 8A* Questions 1, 2, 3.

Painting

The major pieces of woodwork to be painted in any room are doors (including cupboard doors), window frames, sills and skirting boards.

A normal door is about 2·2 m high by 0·6 m to 0·7 m wide; this gives an area of 1·3–1·6 m² per side.

Paint usually covers 12–14 m² to the litre. The area of the door frame and skirting board can be calculated easily, but window frames must be estimated.

Example

If in *Exercises 8A* Question 1, the skirting boards and door frames were 0·025 m thick and the area of window frames to be painted was 2 m² calculate: *a.* the area of wood to be painted, and *b.* the cost of paint, if 1 litre costs 80p and covers 12 m², $\frac{1}{2}$ litre costs 56p.

Solution

Area of door = 2·2 × 0·75 = 1·65 m².
Area of 2 doors = 3·3 m².
Area of skirting = (14m − 2 doors at 0·75 m) = 12·5 m × 0·14 m = 1·75 m².
Area of window frames = 2 m².
Area of door frame (say) 0·5 m².
Total = 7·55 m² approx.
Answer *a.* 7·55 m² to be painted.
Number of litres required = 1 litre.
Answer *b.* Cost = 80p.

Exercises 8C

1. Find:
  i. the area of woodwork to be painted (to nearest 0·5 m²),
  ii. the amount of paint required, and
  iii. the cost of painting the woodwork in the following rooms:
      if 1 litre covers 14 m², and costs £1·05 and $\frac{1}{2}$ litre costs 60p.

	Length	Width	Height	Area and number of doors	Area of window frames, etc.	Height and thickness of skirting
	m	m	m	m	m²	m
a.	5	4	2·5	2·2 × 0·7 (1)	2	0·1 × 0·02
b.	8	4	2·5	2·3 × 0·7 (2)	5	0·1 × 0·02
c.	6	5	2·4	2·2 × 0·7 (1)	2·6	0·1 × 0·02

2. Calculate the amount of paint required to undercoat the woodwork twice, and then gloss paint the woodwork in each of the rooms in *Exercises 8A* No. 2, if undercoat costs 72p per litre and covers 12 m² and gloss paint costs 92p per litre and covers 13 m². If the ½ litre sizes are 40p and 50p respectively, find the cost also. The skirting board and door frames are all 0·025 m thick.

Lawns

Laying turf

Turves are usually sold as pieces 1 m by ⅓ m. The price is usually about £2·75 per 100.

Example

What is the cost of laying a lawn using turves if the area to be covered is 21 m by 9 m?

Solution

Area = 21 × 9 m² = 189 m²

Number of turves = 21 × 9 × 3 = 189 × 3 = 567

Cost = 6 × £2·75 = £16·50.

(*Note.* 600 turves would be ordered.)

Sowing seed

This method of making a lawn probably takes longer, allowing for preparation and growing, but is cheaper. The area to be covered has to be calculated and also the amount of seed required.

Example

If grass seed costs 18p per kg and 0·3 kg covers a square metre, calculate the cost of making a lawn 21 m by 9 m.

Solution

Area = 21 × 9 m² = 189 m².

Amount of seed = 21 × 9 × 0·3 kg = 56·7 kg.

Cost = 56·7 × 18p = £10·21.

Exercises 8D

1. Calculate:

   a. the area in square metres,

b. the cost of covering with turf,

c. the cost of sowing grass seed on plots of land having the following dimensions:

      i. 24 m × 6 m,

      ii. 8 metres square,

      iii. 9 m by 12 m,

iv.   *v.*

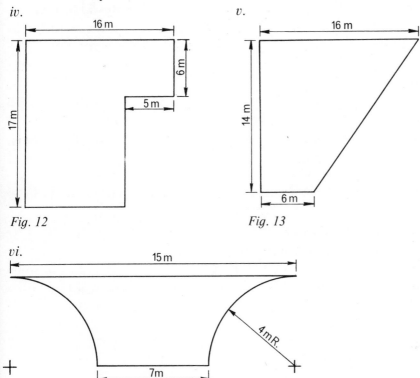

Fig. 12   Fig. 13

vi.

Fig. 14

(Give all answers to the nearest penny.)

Turf prices £2·75 per 100

              £2·25 per 75

              £1·50 per 50

              £1·00 per 25 (smallest quantity)

Grass seed costs 18p per kg and 1 kg covers 4 m^2.

Building materials in the garden

The most common materials used in the garden are:

1. Paving stones, whole or broken.

2. Wall blocks, bricks and stones for building walls.

3. Stone for rockeries.

4. Wood for fences, trellis, gates, sheds and other buildings.

5. Concrete for paths and foundations.

Paving stones vary from 0·25 m square to 1 m long by $\frac{2}{3}$ m wide and the thickness can vary also from 3 cm to 8 cm.

When buying paving stones, choose the variety which will fit best into the area to be covered. The smaller the number of stones, the easier will be the job, but the stones will be heavier than if you had bought smaller ones.

Exercises 8E

Using paving stones measuring 0·5 m by 0·5 m by 0·05 m and costing 23p each, calculate the cost of paving the following areas. For Questions 1–4 only, sketch the area to be paved and show the arrangement of the stones.

1. A path 17 m long by 1 m wide.

2. A backyard 6 m by 4 m.

3. A path 1 m wide all the way round a house which measures 14 m by 10 m.

4. A drive 13 m long by 3·5 m wide. How much would be saved by leaving 0·5 m in the centre unpaved?

5. The table on page 91 shows the cost per 1 000 kg (1 tonne) of stone including delivery charges. Use a large-scale map of England to find the cost of the following deliveries from the nearest depot. There are depots at Maidstone, Hereford and York.

a. 5 000 kg delivered to Sheffield.

b. 141 m² delivered to Lancaster.

c. 3 000 kg delivered to Newport (Shropshire).

d. 5 m² delivered to Nottingham.

e. 18 m² delivered to Tunbridge Wells.

f. 75 m² delivered to Taunton.

g. 7 000 kg delivered to Colchester.

h. 30 m² delivered to Bournemouth.

(Smallest quantity delivered is 5 m². Take 9 m² = 1 000 kg.)

Distance in km measured in a straight line from nearest depot	Prices per 1 000 kg Number of m² or 1 000 kg ordered			
	1–18 m² 0–2000 kg	*19–36* m² 2000–4000 kg	*37–54* m² 4000–6000 kg	*55* m² *and over more than* 6000 kg
	£	£	£	£
0–24	1·00	0·95	0·90	0·80
25–48	1·02½	0·97	0·92	0·82½
49–80	1·05	0·99	0·94	0·85
81–112	1·07½	1·01	0·96	0·87½
113–160	1·10	1·05	0·98	0·90
161–192	1·12½	1·07	1·00	0·92½
193–224	1·15	1·09	1·02	0·95
225–256	1·17½	1·11	1·04	0·97½
257–288	1·20	1·13	1·07	1·00
289–320	1·22½	1·15	1·10	1·02½
Over 320	1·25	1·20	1·15	1·05

9 Heating and lighting

Electricity

Reading the meter

There are various patterns of electricity meter, but all have six dials and should be read* starting with the highest quantity, i.e. the 10000 dial, and working towards the smallest dial. The $\frac{1}{10}$ dial is not used for taking a meter reading.

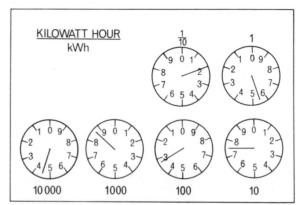

Fig. 15

* It should be noted that different manufacturers produce electricity meters the dials of which are numbered in different directions; that is, one manufacturer may make a meter with the 10000 dial numbered clockwise as in Fig. 16 and another manufacturer produce a meter with a 10000 dial numbered anti-clockwise as in Fig. 15. The way in which this is done is of no importance. What should be noted carefully, however, is that adjacent dials are always numbered in alternate directions.

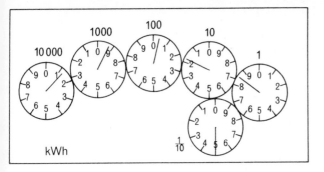

Fig. 16

The numbers 10000, 1000, 100, 10 and 1 refer to the divisions on the face of the dial.

Always read the smaller of the two numbers when the pointer lies between them, except when it is between 9 and 0, in which case read 9.

First study the examples below, then read the dials shown

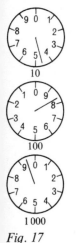

The reading is 4 tens   = 40 units

The reading is 8 hundreds = 800 units

The reading is 9 thousands = 9000 units

Fig. 17

Exercises 9A
Read the dials shown below. Take care to say whether the readings are in tens, hundreds, etc.

1.   The reading is . . . . =   units

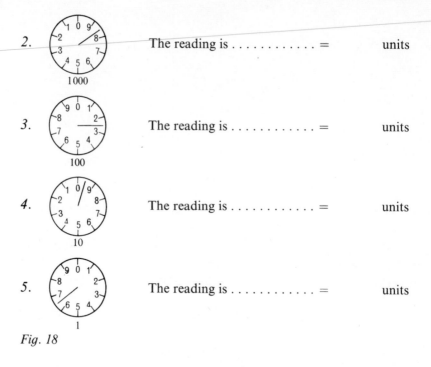

2. The reading is . . . . =   units

3. The reading is . . . . =   units

4. The reading is . . . . =   units

5. The reading is . . . . =   units

Fig. 18

6. Now read the meters shown at the start of this chapter.

Recording the meter-reading

When the electricity meter inspector calls he will read the meter and record this information in a book or on a card. The electricity board will then decide how many units of electricity you have used since the meter was last read.

The information is recorded on a card like the one shown below:

Name. . . . .
Address . . . .

Date	Reading	Consumption
12th January	00000	
27th April	01690	
16th July	02750	
19th October	03672	
14th January	05891	
17th April	07743	
25th July	09137	

Exercises 9B

1. Copy the table on page 94 and calculate the number of units used each quarter. Put these numbers in the column headed 'consumption'.

2. Examine your answer to Question 1 and note the variation in consumption between quarters. Explain why the consumption varies in this way.

3. Read your own meter daily for a week and weekly for a quarter and record the information in your book. Try to account for the fluctuations in both daily and weekly consumption.

Fill in your table like this and complete the remarks column.

Day	Date	Time	Meter reading	Units used	Weather	Remarks
Mon	11th Oct	22.00	76413	8	Fine	—
Tue	12th Oct	22.00	76421	8	Fine	—
Wed	13th Oct	22.00	76430	9	Pleasant	—
Thur	14th Oct	22.00	76456	26	Bitterly cold	—
Fri	15th Oct	22.00	76475	19	Cool	Bath night
Sat	16th Oct	22.00	76486	11	Nice day	Had lunch out
Sun	17th Oct	22.00	76508	22	Cool	Cooked lunch
Mon	18th Oct	22.00	76523	15	Cool	Washing and ironing
Tue	19th Oct	22.00	76531	8	Pleasant	—

4. What appears to be an average day's consumption of electricity if no special appliances are being used and the weather is fine?

5. Explain the increase in consumption on Thursday, 14th October; Friday, 15th October, Sunday, 17th October, and Monday, 18th October.

Units of electricity

The unit of electricity measured by the meters described earlier in this chapter is a standard set up by the Board of Trade. Its proper name is a *kilowatt hour* and is the amount of work done by 1000 watts (1 kilowatt) of electricity in 1 hour.

Most appliances are marked to show their rate of consuming electricity, together with certain other items of important information.

If electricity costs 1·1p* per unit (1000 watts for 1 hour) the cost of running an electric fire marked 2 kW (2000 watts) for *one* hour will be

---

* Electricity Boards have charged fractions of a penny e.g. 2·1*d*, 0·8*d* for some years now, in fact, long before the introduction of decimal currency. Consequently although it is not common practice to show decimal fractions of a new penny it is standard practice in this case.

$$\frac{2000}{1000} \times 1 \cdot 1p = 2 \cdot 2p \text{ OR } 2 \text{ kW} \times 1 \text{ hour at } 1 \cdot 1p/kWh = 2 \times 1 \times 1 \cdot 1p = 2 \cdot 2p.$$

Example 1

If electricity costs 1·25p per unit, find the cost of running an iron marked 400 watts for $1\frac{1}{4}$ hours.

Solution

$$\text{The cost will be } \frac{400}{1000} \times 1\tfrac{1}{4} \times 1 \cdot 25p = 0 \cdot 675p.$$

Example 2

How long will it take this iron (400 watts) to consume one unit of electricity?

Solution

$$\text{It will take } \frac{1000}{400} \text{ hours} = 2\tfrac{1}{2} \text{ hours.}$$

Example 3

If electricity costs 2p per unit, for how long can a 2 kW fire be used for 18p (2 kW = 2000 watts).

Solution

$$\text{Cost per hour} = \frac{2000}{1000} \times 2p = 4p.$$

$$\therefore \text{ The fire can be used for } \frac{18p}{4p} \text{ hours} = 4\tfrac{1}{2} \text{ hours.}$$

Exercises 9C

1. Copy out and complete the table below. In *g* and *h* calculate the size in watts and kilowatts of the appliance.

	Size of appliance	Cost per unit	Time in use	Number of units used	Cost of electricity used
		p			p
a.	3 kW fire	2·40	1 hour	?	?
b.	500 watt iron	1·60	45 minutes	?	?
c.	2500 watt electric kettle	2·25	?	?	3
d.	3 kW fire	?	3 hours	?	18
e.	1250 watt toaster	1·75	?	?	$3\frac{1}{2}$
f.	3 kW immersion heater	?	1 hour 20 minutes	?	10
g.	?	0·90	2 hours	?	4·5
h.	?	0·88	70 minutes	?	2·31

2. Make a list of the electrical appliances in your home. Look for the plate which is usually on the back or underside of the appliance and from it find the size of the appliance. From an electricity account find the cost of a unit of electricity.

Finally calculate the cost of running the appliance for an hour.

The electricity account (or bill)

The charges for electricity vary from one area to another and also between domestic and industrial consumers. The exact charge can be found on the electricity account.

Most electricity boards have a tariff, that is a scale of charges, in two parts. The first part is a lump sum sometimes determined by the number of rooms in the house and at other times just a predetermined figure. The second part is a charge based on the number of units consumed at a specific price per unit.

Examples of some different tariffs are given below.

A. A fixed charge of £1·40 and all units charged at 0·9p per unit.

B. The first 44 units at 2·5p per unit and the remainder at 1·0p per unit.

Example

Calculate the cost of 1500 units on:

   i. tariff A.

   ii. tariff B.

Solution

   i. Tariff A.

      Cost = £1·40 + 1500 × 0·9p = £1·40 + £13·50 = £14·90.

   ii. Tariff B.

      Cost = 44 × 2·5p + 1456 × 1p = £1·10 + £14·56 = £15·66.

Exercises 9D

   1. Using the meter card on page 94 and each of the tariffs A and B above, calculate the quarterly charges for electricity for the six quarters shown.

   2. Draw a graph for each of the tariffs A and B and find for what consumption of electricity the cost is the same on each tariff. What is this cost?

Off-peak tariffs for domestic electricity supplies

Most electricity boards offer a variety of tariffs which apply to electricity supplied at 'off-peak' times. The boards stipulate that the supply is used *a.* during the specified hours only,

b. for storage heaters, floor warming and similar devices.

The consumer must agree that the installation shall be used on the agreed supply only.

Some off-peak tariffs are shown below:

Tariff	Times available	Cost
X	Throughout the year from 23.00 to 07.00	0·35p per unit
Y	Throughout the year from 23.00 to 07.00 and from 13.00 to 16.00	0·40p per unit
Z	November–March inclusive from 19.00 to 07.00 and from 13.00 to 16.00 and from 19.00 Friday to 07.00 Monday April–October no restrictions	0·52p per unit

There is a quarterly charge of £·055 for the equipment installed.

Exercises 9E

1. What is the quarterly bill for off-peak electricity using each tariff if 8000 units are consumed?

2. Describe one advantage of each of the tariffs X, Y, and Z.

3. A man used 2100 units on Tariff A in the quarter January–March 1968. Find how much this electricity cost. During the summer he had storage heaters installed and his bill for January–March 1969 was

1400 units on Tariff A.

950 units on Tariff Y.

Find the cost of electricity in this quarter. Include the quarterly charge of £0·55 with Tariff Y.

Gas

Reading the meter

Like the electricity meters shown on pages 92 and 93 there are various patterns of gas meter. Unlike the electricity meters there are no dials for units. From the dials you read the first four figures of a five-figure number, e.g. if the dials show 1, 2, 3, 4 the reading would be 12340 cubic metres.

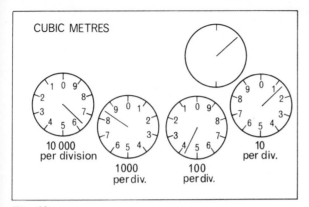

CUBIC METRES

10 000
per division

1000
per div.

100
per div.

10
per div.

Fig. 19

Read the meter above in exactly the same way as you read the electricity meters earlier. Remember when the pointer lies between two figures always read the smaller, except when it lies between 0 and 9, then read 9.

Exercises 9F

1. Copy the meters shown below into your book and write down the reading beside each diagram.

Fig. 20   April 1969

Fig. 21   July 1969

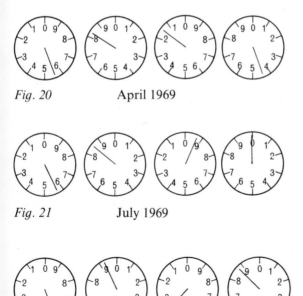

Fig. 22   October 1969

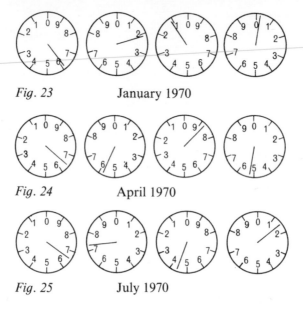

Fig. 23   January 1970

Fig. 24   April 1970

Fig. 25   July 1970

2. Calculate the consumption of gas in the periods:
a. April to July 1969,
b. July to October 1969,
c. October 1969 to January 1970,
d. January 1970 to April 1970,
e. April to July 1970.

3. If the consumption in the six previous quarters had been October 1967–January 1968, 1380 m³; January 1968–April 1968, 1420 m³; April 1968–July 1968, 650 m³; July 1968–October 1968, 540 m³; October 1968–January 1969, 1700 m³; January 1969–April 1969, 1670 m³, draw a graph showing consumption per quarter from January 1968 to April 1969.

4. If the householder had gas-fired central heating installed during this period:
a. say when you think this was carried out,
b. calculate approximately the increase in consumption per winter quarter (October to January and January to April) due to running the central heating.

5. The graph opposite shows the consumption of gas by months for a house using gas for the majority of its heating and cooking.
a. Find the total consumption of gas in hundreds of m³.
b. Divide the year into four quarters (January–March, etc.) and work out the quarterly consumption of gas.

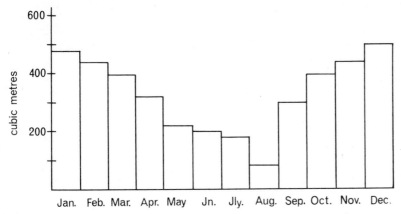

Fig. 26

The price of gas
Different gas boards charge different prices for the gas they supply. These
charges are called a 'tariff'.

Domestic tariff A

Therms supplied per quarter	Price per therm	Number of m^3	Price per $100\ m^3$
First 10 therms	$7\frac{1}{2}$p per therm	50	£1·50
All over 10 therms	$4\frac{1}{2}$p per therm	—	90p

A therm is the amount of heat generated by the gas and will vary from
board to board.

Board A produces gas which gives 1 therm to each 5 m³. Gas boards are
enforced by Act of Parliament to specify the heating power of their gas
and to charge according to the heating power supplied and not just on the
number of cubic metres.

It is easier for the householder to understand how many cubic metres he
has used and so for the convenience of both parties (board and consumer)
the heating power (more correctly called 'declared heating value') is kept as
constant as possible.

Example 1
What will be charged for: *a.* 10 therms, *b.* 15 therms, *c.* 22 therms?

Solution
a. $10 \times 7\frac{1}{2}$p $= 75$p.
b. $10 \times 7\frac{1}{2}$p $+ 5 \times 4\frac{1}{2}$p $= 75 + 22\frac{1}{2}$p $= 97\frac{1}{2}$p.
c. $10 \times 7\frac{1}{2}$p $+ 12 \times 4\frac{1}{2}$p $= £1·29$.

Example 2

In this tariff there are 10 therms for each 50 m³, that is 1 therm is equivalent to 5 m³.

    a. How many cubic metres will give: *i.* 7 therms, *ii.* 15 therms?

    b. A customer used *i.* 700 m³, *ii.* 230 m³. In each case how many therms were supplied?

    c. In all four cases above, what was the cost of the gas supplied?

Solution

    a. If 1 therm is equivalent to 5 m³

        i. then 7 therms are equivalent to $7 \times 5 = 35$ m³,

        ii. 15 therms are equivalent to $15 \times 5 = 75$ m³.

    b. 700 cubic metres give $\dfrac{700}{5} = 140$ therms,

        230 cubic metres give $\dfrac{230}{5} = 46$ therms.

    c.   7 therms cost $7 \times 7\frac{1}{2}\text{p} = 52\frac{1}{2}\text{p}$,

        15 therms cost $10 \times 7\frac{1}{2}\text{p} + 5 \times 4\frac{1}{2}\text{p} = 87\frac{1}{2}\text{p}$,

    140 therms cost $10 \times 7\frac{1}{2}\text{p} + 130 \times 4\frac{1}{2}\text{p} = £6 \cdot 10$,

     46 therms cost $10 \times 7\frac{1}{2}\text{p} + 36 \times 4\frac{1}{2}\text{p} = £2 \cdot 37$.

Exercises 9G

    1. Find the cost of: *a.* 8 therms, *b.* 18 therms, *c.* 28 therms using Tariff A.

    2. How many m³ will give: *a.* 9 therms, *b.* 21 therms?

    3. If a customer uses: *i.* 500 m³, *ii.* 1270 m³ state how many therms were supplied and what the charge was in each case.

    Three further tariffs are shown below.

Domestic tariff B

A standard charge of £1·35 and all gas consumed is charged at the rate of 3p per m³.

    The same board also has two tariffs for larger customers:

Tariff C—a standard charge of £3·35 and all gas consumed is charged at the rate of 2·7p per m³.

Tariff D—a standard charge of £9·35 and all gas consumed is charged at the rate of 2·5p per m³.

    The declared heating value of this board's gas is 0·16 therm per m³.

Example

  a. Calculate the number of m³ which are equivalent to 1 therm.

  b. If the board supplies 1 000 m³ of gas, what is the heating value of this quantity of gas in therms?

  c. If the board supplies sufficient gas to produce 12 therms, how many cubic metres of gas is this?

  d. Using each of the Tariffs B, C and D in turn, calculate the cost of 750 m³ of gas.

Solution

  a. If 0·16 therm is equivalent to 1 m³, then 1 therm is equivalent to

$$\frac{1}{0·16} = \frac{100}{16} = 6·25 \text{ m}^3,$$

  b. 1 m³ provides 0·16 therm

  ∴ 1 000 m³ provides 1 000 × 0·16 = 160 therms,

  c. 1 therm is equivalent to 6·25 m³

  ∴ 12 therms are equivalent to 12 × 6·25 m³ = 75 m³,

  d. On Tariff B 750 m³ cost £1·35 + 750 × 3p = £23·85,

  On Tariff C 750 m³ cost £3·35 + 750 × 2·7p = £23·60,

  On Tariff D 750 m³ cost £9·35 + 750 × 2·5p = £28·15.

Exercises 9H

  1. Using Tariff B, what is the heating value in therms and cost of

  a. 100 m³, *b.* 700 m³, *c.* 1200 m³?

  2. Using Tariffs B, C and D in turn, calculate:

  a. the cost of 540 m³ of gas,

  b. how many cubic metres are obtained for twice the amount found in *a*?

  3. An average household consumes about 100 therms. Calculate the cost using Tariffs B, C and D and determine which of the tariffs is the best:

  a. for the average consumer,

  b. for the consumer who uses less than the average,

  c. for the consumer who uses more than the average.

  4. By drawing graphs of each tariff, plotting number of m³ used horizontally and cost vertically, find:

  a. the number of units for which the cost on:

    i. Tariffs A and B,

    ii. Tariffs B and C,

    iii. Tariffs B and D,

    iv. Tariffs C and D are the same;

b. the cost at each of these points;
c. which of Tariffs A or B is the more favourable for the small consumer;
d. the consumption above which a large consumer should choose to use:
  i. Tariff C, rather than B,
  ii. Tariff D, rather than C or B.

10 Household expenses

Many of the expenses which householders have to meet have been described in the preceding chapters, insurance and assurance, house purchase, rent and rates, house maintenance and heating and lighting.

However, there are many other bills such as the regular purchase of food and groceries, and the purchase of larger items such as furniture, cycles and radios.

Household bills

Copy out the items in Column A, find the prices at your local grocer (G) and at a supermarket (S).

A	Weight of	G	S	A	Weight of	G	S
Tea				Currants			
Cocoa				Sultanas			
Coffee				Jam			
Sugar				Marmalade			
Bacon				Jelly			
Lamb joint				Custard powder (tin)			
Beef joint				Corn flakes			
Butter				Porridge oats			
Margarine				Small tin soup			
Cooking fat				Packet soap powder			
Large baked beans				Washing-up liquid			
Tin garden peas				Toothpaste			
Self-raising flour				Orange squash			
Golden syrup				Tomato ketchup			

Exercises 10A

1. Calculate the weekly bills in the following cases at both a small grocer and a supermarket—use your own prices and quantities.

For a family of two	For a family of four	For a large family
Tea	Tea	Tea
Coffee	Coffee	Sugar
Sugar	Sugar	Cocoa
Cocoa	Bacon	Bacon
Bacon	Margarine	Margarine
Butter	Butter	Butter
Margarine	Cooking fat	Cooking fat
Cooking fat	Potatoes	Potatoes
Potatoes	2 tins peas	4 tins peas
2 tins peas	1 tin tomato soup	6 large tins baked beans
2 large tins baked beans	1 dozen eggs	3 dozen eggs
2 dozen eggs	Self-raising flour	2 tins syrup
Jam	Currants	Beef
Pork sausages	Milk	Lamb
Milk	Bottle orange squash	Large corn flakes
Lamb	Large toothpaste	Washing-up liquid
Large corn flakes	Jam	Milk

2. Select the quantities and groceries you would buy if you wished to spend about £2 on food and had to prepare all your own meals except a midday meal Monday to Friday.

3. Comment on the difference in prices at the small grocer and at the supermarket. What are the differences in service and choice at the two types of shop? Where does your family do the majority of its shopping? Indicate the amounts spent weekly at the different shops. Why does your family use these shops?

Invoices, delivery notes, receipts and discount

Many shopkeepers will give their customers a piece of paper indicating how much money the customer has to pay. Such a piece of paper is called a bill or invoice. If you order goods such as furniture, large electrical appliances or garden fixtures and machinery, they will be delivered by the shopkeeper. Often you will receive a delivery note at the same time. The invoice is sent later.

When you pay the shopkeeper he will give you a receipt.

The transactions between yourself and the shopkeeper are similar to those between the wholesaler (or supplier) and the shopkeeper.

The shopkeeper orders goods. They are sent with a delivery note. Later the shopkeeper receives an invoice. Often the wholesaler will allow the shopkeeper to reduce the amount owing by a given percentage to enable the shopkeeper to make a profit. Such a reduction is called a discount (a 'trade' discount). In certain circumstances the shopkeeper may allow you a discount if he wishes to sell goods quickly, or if they are damaged or soiled, or if you spend a lot of money there and sometimes if you pay cash (a 'cash' discount). Cash discounts are usually given for prompt payment of accounts. For example, '$2\frac{1}{2}\%$ one month' means that the total amount owing may be reduced by $2\frac{1}{2}$ per cent if the account is settled within one month of the date shown on the invoice.

Example 1
A wholesaler sells stockings at 33p a pair to a shopkeeper. He informs the shopkeeper that he should deduct a discount of $33\frac{1}{3}$ per cent before settling his bill and sell the stockings at 33p a pair. How much will the shopkeeper
   a. pay for 60 pairs of stockings, and
   b. receive for those stockings when he has sold them all?

Solution
   a. $33\frac{1}{3}$ per cent of 33p = 11p. The discount is 11p.
       ∴ The price paid to the wholesaler is 22p a pair.
       Total price paid to wholesaler = $60 \times 22p = £13 \cdot 20$.
   b. Price paid to shopkeeper = $60 \times 33p = £19 \cdot 80$.

Example 2
If the wholesaler gives a further 5 per cent discount for prompt payment how much would the shopkeeper then pay?

Solution
$\frac{5}{100} \times £13 \cdot 20 = 66p$.
∴ Price paid to the wholesaler = $£13 \cdot 20 - £0 \cdot 66 = £12 \cdot 54$.

Exercises 10B

Many firms allow 5 per cent discount for payment within one month and $2\frac{1}{2}$ per cent discount for payment within two months.
   1. Find the discount and actual payment on each of these bills.

	Nature of goods	Date purchased	Date of payment	Price
				£
a.	Lawnmower	June 7th	June 14th	7·50
b.	Wheelbarrow	June 9th	July 10th	4·40
c.	Trellis	June 12th	August 15th	6·45
d.	Garden tools	June 14th	August 10th	7·40

2. An outfitter buys goods at 20 per cent below the list price (i.e. the price at which they are to be sold); he is also allowed the discount shown above for prompt payment. Find out how much he pays for the following goods:

	Nature of goods	Quantity	Price	Date bought	Date of payment
a.	Shirts	36	£1·75 each	Sept 16th	Sept 30th
b.	Socks	120 pairs	24p pair	Sept 27th	Oct 30th
c.	Pyjamas	36 pairs	$97\frac{1}{2}$p pair	Nov 25th	Jan 30th
d.	Handkerchiefs	144	3p each	Nov 16th	Feb 26th
e.	Skirts	18	£2·75 each	Jan 27th	Feb 26th

3. What does a bill or invoice look like? Draw one in your book. Try to obtain some from local shops.

4. What is a statement? To whom is a statement sent and when? What is the difference between a statement and an invoice?

5. Who gives discount? Why is discount given?

6. A 'sale' is a form of giving discount. Record in your books a series of sale notices and the prices before and after reduction. For example: 'January Sales 25 per cent off all suits'.
This suit reduced to £7·50 from £9·99.

Depreciation

Large items of furniture, cars, motor-cycles and electrical goods often lose some of their cash value after they have been purchased.

For instance, a new car might cost £700 and by the time it is one year old it is probably worth about £600. This deterioration in the value of goods like the articles mentioned above and also machinery and even some types of building is called *depreciation*.

Example

A car valued at £1000 depreciates by 10 per cent of its value in the previous year. How much is it worth at the end of the first, second and third years?

Solution

Initial value £1000

Depreciation during first year	= 10 per cent of £1000	= £100
Value at end of first year	= £1000 − £100	= £900
Depreciation during second year	= 10 per cent of £900	= £90
Value at end of second year	= £900 − £90	= £810
Depreciation during third year	= 10 per cent of £810	= £81
Value at end of third year	= £810 − £81	= £729

Note the following simpler way of arriving at the answer:

Initial value £1000

Value at end of first year $= \dfrac{9}{10} \times 1000 = £900.$

Value at end of second year $= \dfrac{9}{10} \times 900 = £810.$

Value at end of third year $= \dfrac{9}{10} \times 810 = £729.$

Exercises 10C

Find the value at the end of the first, second and third years of the following:

1. Car value £650, depreciation 10 per cent per annum.
2. Motor-cycle value £250, depreciation 20 per cent per annum.
3. Washing machine value £120, depreciation 30 per cent per annum.
4. Television set value £84, depreciation 10 per cent per annum.
5. Agricultural machinery value £3500, depreciation 15 per cent per annum.
6. Workshop value £5000, depreciation $12\frac{1}{2}$ per cent per annum.

Hire purchase

The system of hire purchase enables you to obtain goods without paying for them on the spot. The payments can usually be spread over a period up to three years. Spreading the payments can be very helpful if a person wishes to furnish a home, but it can also lead to difficulties and unhappiness if too many articles are bought in this way.

Exercises 10D

On the next page are typical advertisements to be found in shop windows, in the newspaper and on television. Study each advertisement and answer Questions 1–5 in each case.

a.

SPECIAL OFFER
3 piece suite £119·50
Deposit 10 per cent +
32 weekly payments
of £3·96

1. What amount would you pay if you paid cash down?

2. What are the hire purchase terms? (remember the deposit).

3. What total sum do you pay if you buy it on HP?

4. By how much does the hire purchase price exceed the cash price?

5. Express the difference between the two prices:

   i. as a fraction

  ii. as a percentage

of the cash price.

b.

EASY TERMS
REFRIGERATOR
Cash Price £59·95
Deposit £9 + 12 monthly
payments of £4·95

c.

TEAK BEDROOM SUITE
£102·90
OR
DEPOSIT £15·65
and 12 monthly payments of £8·15

Find the answers to these questions on *hire purchase*. What are the advantages and disadvantages of buying goods on hire purchase both to the customer and the shopkeeper? What deposit is required before goods can be removed from the shop?

Find some examples of repayment periods locally and suggest which of these are most common. How is the interest calculated on a hire purchase loan? How are the repayments calculated?

Work out the total interest and comment on the 'actual' rate of interest charged. (Note if repayments take 2 years, half of the original loan has been repaid by the end of the first year.)

Exercises 10E
Study the following table of information and note the difference between the cash price and the total hire purchase price of the two items worked for you. Complete the table in your books and comment afterwards on the difference between cash and hire purchase prices. Express this difference as a percentage of the cash price.

Item	Cash price	Deposit	Number of payments	Interval	Amount	Total hire purchase price
	£	£			£	£
1. Stereogram	59·85	6·45	24	Monthly	2·67	24 × 2·67 + 6·45 = 70·53
2. Cycle	29·45	4·95	12	Monthly	2·56	12 × 2·56 + 4·95 = 35·67
3. Gas cooker	68·25	6·92½	16	Quarterly	4·65	
4. Electric cooker	56·72	5·72	16	Quarterly	3·86	
5. Binoculars	6·97	0·87	9	Monthly	0·78	

Example 1

In the first case the cash price is £59·85.

Deposit £6·45   balance £53·40.

Hire purchase charge is 10 per cent per annum.

Solution

£53·40 × 10 per cent for 2 years = £53·40 × $\dfrac{\cancel{10} \times \cancel{2}}{\cancel{100}\ \underset{5}{\cancel{10}}}$ = £10·68.

Hire purchase balance = £53·40 + £10·68 = £64·08, that is 24 monthly payments of £2·67.

The hire purchase charge is 20 per cent (one-fifth) of the oustanding cash balance. The difference in prices is £70·53 − £59·85 = £10·68 expressed as a percentage per annum is

$$\frac{10·68}{59·85} \times \frac{100}{2} = 8·92 \text{ per cent.}$$

(Note division by 2 because the repayments are over 2 years.)

Example 2

A bicycle costing £29·45 may be bought on hire purchase by putting down a deposit of £4·95 and repaying the balance, together with hire purchase charges, by 12 monthly instalments of £2·56.

 a. What is the total hire purchase price?

 b. What is the difference between the hire purchase and cash prices?

 c. What is this difference expressed as a percentage of the cash price per annum?

Solution

　　a. Total hire purchase price = £4·95 + (12 × £2·56) = £4·95 + £30·72
= £35·67.

　　b. The difference between the hire purchase and cash prices is £35·67 −
£29·45, that is £6·22.

　　c. This difference expressed as a percentage is

$$\frac{6·22}{29·45} \times 100 \text{ per cent} = 21·1 \text{ per cent.}$$

Exercises 10F

　　1. If the total hire purchase price of an electrical appliance was £46·11
and there were 16 quarterly repayments of £2·69, what deposit is required?
The cash price was £39·50; calculate the difference between these prices as a
percentage per annum of the cash price.

　　2. A child's cycle can be bought for £12·67 cash, or 12 monthly payments of £1·13 and a deposit of £1·42. What is the hire purchase charge?

　　3. A battery-charging set can be purchased for a deposit of £5·12 and
9 monthly payments of £3·18. What is the hire purchase price? If the hire
purchase price exceeds the cash price by £3·81 what is the cash price?

　　4. A teenager spends 14p a day 6 days a week for 48 weeks of the year on
bus fares. If he put down the deposit of £4·96 on a bicycle and made
12 monthly payments of £2·67, find out how much he saves in a year by
buying and using the cycle instead of travelling by bus.

Exercises 10G

　　1. Here are some of the first questions you will be asked when you try to
buy goods on hire purchase. In each case give the reason why the question
is asked.

　　a. Your full name.

　　b. Present address and the time you have lived there.

　　c. Your age.

　　d. The name and address of your employer.

　　e. The name and address of a guarantor or reference.

　　2. What is meant by:

　　a. a guarantor,

　　b. a deposit,

　　c. an instalment?

3. Obtain a hire purchase proposal form from a local shop and study it. Find all the questions and words used in Questions 1 and 2 above.

4. List another six questions which are to be found on hire purchase proposal forms.

5. What happens to the goods if a purchaser does not make his hire purchase payments on time?

11 Holidays

Timetables and journeys

Here are some suggestions which will be useful in using timetables and planning journeys.

1. Always try to start from some fixed point or points, such as 'must be in Aberdeen by 19.50'. This probably means working backwards through the timetables, having found a train or bus which arrives in Aberdeen at or before 19.50.

2. Make due allowances for changing trains or buses or from one form of transport to another, particularly crossing London and other big cities or making your way from a bus or train terminal to an air or sea port.

24-hour clock

Most timetables both in this country and on the Continent are printed using the 24-hour day, i.e. 2.0 p.m. is 14.00 hours or just 14.00; 3.10 a.m. is 03.10 hours; twenty-five to eight in the evening is 19.35 hours. In some timetables the point is left out and this last time would be given as 1935.

Exercises 11A

Convert the following to times on the 24-hour clock;

1a. ten to eight in the morning, *b.* midnight, *c.* 6.30 p.m., *d.* midday, *e.* five past midnight, *f.* five minutes before midnight, *g.* quarter to ten in the evening.

2. Write these times using a.m. and p.m.:
a. 07.40, *b.* 19.36, *c.* 00.30, *d.* 15.45, *e.* 19.20, *f.* 21.50, *g.* 13.10.

3. A coach leaves London on a 189 km journey to Bristol, at 21.45 hours. The journey including stops takes $3\frac{1}{2}$ hours.
   a. What time does the coach reach Bristol?
   b. What is the average speed for the journey?
   c. If the coach stops for half an hour, two hours after leaving London
      i. at what times does it stop and restart its journey,
     ii. what is its average speed whilst travelling?

4. Make out a timetable for a coach which leaves Edinburgh at 21.15, reaches Newcastle $2\frac{1}{4}$ hours later, Durham 1 hour 10 minutes after leaving Newcastle, and York 1 hour 50 minutes after leaving Newcastle. Allow ten minutes wait at each stop.

If the distance from Edinburgh to York is 306 km, find the average speed of the journey.

Train timetables and costs

The following is an extract from a railway timetable:

Timetable X

		A	B
Manchester—Piccadilly	dep.	10.00	10.25
Stockport	dep.	10.10	10.36
Liverpool—Lime Street	dep.		10.05
Crewe	dep.		11.18
Wolverhampton—Low Level	dep.	12.20	12.40
Birmingham—Snow Hill	dep.	12.43	13.04
Southampton	dep.	15.55	16.37
West Cowes	arr.	17.25	18.10
Bournemouth Central	arr.	16.47	17.35

Exercises 11B

  1a. How long did each train take for the journey:
     i. from Manchester to Stockport,
    ii. from Manchester to Wolverhampton,
   iii. from Manchester to Birmingham,
    iv. from Manchester to Southampton,
     v. from Birmingham to Southampton,
    vi. from Manchester to Bournemouth,
   vii. from Southampton to Bournemouth?
  b. How long do you think it takes to get to the Isle of Wight from Southampton?

c. These two trains only run on one day each week. Which day do you think it is? Give reasons for your answer.

2. Using the same timetable:

a. Do you think a man returning from Bournemouth to Manchester on a train leaving Bournemouth at 10.00 hours should be in Manchester before 18.00 ?

b. If Manchester to Birmingham is 132 km,

Manchester to Southampton is 352 km,

Manchester to Bournemouth is 396 km,

calculate to one place of decimals the average speed of the trains:

i. from Manchester to Birmingham,

ii. from Birmingham to Southampton,

iii. from Southampton to Bournemouth,

iv. for the whole journey.

c. If the return fare from Manchester to Bournemouth was £6, calculate to the nearest $\frac{1}{10}$ penny the cost of this journey per mile.

d. Suggest places at which the coaches from Liverpool would join the coaches from Manchester.

e. Use your atlas to find:

i. other stations from which passengers might come to join this train,

ii. where passengers might go when they arrive at West Cowes,

iii. if they were to stay on the train at Bournemouth where is it likely to go next?

Timetable Y

Kilometres from Waterloo											
0	London Waterloo	dep	11.30	12.30	12.35	14.30	15.35	16.35		19.30	21.20
78	Basingstoke	arr	12.35				16.41			20.34	22.23
		dep	12.36				16.42			20.35	22.24
94	Micheldever	dep					17.00			20.55	
107	Winchester City	dep	13.04			15.51	17.13	17.58		21.09	22.52
119	Eastleigh	arr					17.25			21.21	
		dep					17.26			21.23	
128	Southampton Central	arr	13.26	14.03	14.19	16.11	17.40	18.19		21.37	23.12
		dep	13.29	14.05	14.20	16.12	17.42	18.21		21.42	23.13
150	Brockenhurst	arr	13.50		14.43	16.35	18.06	18.44		22.05	23.36
		dep	13.51		14.44	16.36	18.08	18.46		22.06	23.37
158	New Milton	dep	14.03				18.21			22.18	23.52
163	Hinton Admiral	dep	14.10								
168	Christchurch	dep	14.19			16.54	18.32			22.28	00.02
171	Pokesdown	dep	14.25				18.39			22.35	
173	Boscombe	dep					18.43				
174	Bournemouth Central	arr	14.30	14.48	15.07	17.07	18.47	19.10		22.40	00.11

3. What is the distance between:
a. Waterloo and Southampton,
b. Waterloo and Bournemouth,
c. Winchester and Christchurch,
d. Boscombe and Micheldever,
e. New Milton and Eastleigh,
f. Pokesdown and Winchester?

4. Find the time that these trains arrive at the stations named below:
a. 11.30 from Waterloo at Bournemouth,
b. 15.51 from Winchester at Brockenhurst,
c. 16.41 from Basingstoke at Southampton,
d. 21.42 from Southampton at Christchurch.

5. Find the time taken for each of the trains to make:
a. the journey from Waterloo to Southampton,
b. the journey from Southampton to Bournemouth,
c. the journey from Waterloo to Bournemouth.

6. Calculate the average speed of each of the trains in kilometres per hour over the complete journey (give your answer correct to the nearest 0·5 km/h).

7. Explain the variation in stopping time at Southampton.

8. At what time does a passenger have to leave London in order to be
a. in Bournemouth by 17.30,   *b.* in Bournemouth before midnight,
c. in Bournemouth before 15.00, *d.* in Christchurch by 16.00,
e. in Southampton by 18.15,   *f.* in Brockenhurst by 17.30?

Foreign currencies

The current rates of exchange can be found in many national newspapers.
    Below are listed approximate rates operating in 1970.

£1 sterling =	Austria	61·5 schillings	Italy	1 500 lire
	Belgium	120 francs	Spain	166 pesetas
	Canada	2·56 dollars	Sweden	12·3 kroner
	France	13·3 francs	Switzerland	10·2 francs
	Germany	9·3 marks	U.S.A.	2·38 dollars
	Holland	8·6 guilders	U.S.S.R.	12 roubles

Exercises 11C

1. Convert the following sums of English money (sterling) into
   a. French francs,
   b. Italian lire,
   c. American dollars:
      i. £25, ii. £120·50, iii. £8·37½, iv. £19·62, v. £7·14, iv. £3·87.

2. Convert the following sums into sterling:
   a. 111 Russian roubles,
   b. 1230 Austrian schillings,
   c. 624 Belgian francs,
   d. 67·32 Swiss francs,
   e. 1000 Dutch guilders (to nearest penny).

Metric measures

These have been in use throughout Europe and are now being adopted more and more in the United Kingdom.

The basic unit of length is the metre (m). Large distances are measured in kilometres (km) and short lengths in centimetres (cm) or millimetres (mm).

$$1000 \text{ mm} = 1 \text{ m}$$
$$100 \text{ cm} = 1 \text{ m}$$
$$1000 \text{ m} = 1 \text{ km}$$

Similarly the cubic metre (m³) is the basic unit of volume. This is very large for everyday use so the cubic decimetre (dm³) or litre (l) and the cubic centimetre (cm³) are commonly used.

$$1000 \text{ dm}^3 = 1 \text{ m}^3$$
$$1 \text{ dm}^3 = 1 \text{ litre}$$
$$1000 \text{ cm}^3 = 1 \text{ dm}^3 \text{ (or 1 litre)}$$

Conversion between metric and English units should not be needed very often. If accurate conversions are required exact conversion factors should be used, but the following are roughly equivalent:

$$1 \text{ km} = \tfrac{5}{8} \text{ mile}$$
$$1 \text{ litre} = 1\tfrac{3}{4} \text{ pints}$$

Example
If the petrol tank of a car holds 7 gallons, what is the capacity of the tank in litres?

Solution

$1\frac{3}{4}$ pints $= 1$ litre

$\therefore$ 56 pints $= \dfrac{1 \times 56}{1\frac{3}{4}} = \dfrac{56 \times 4}{7} = 32$ litres (approximately).

Use approximate conversions in the following questions.

Exercises 11D

1. During a motoring holiday in Europe the following signposts were passed:

Calais to Paris	108 km,
Paris to Frankfurt	544 km,
Frankfurt to Berlin	768 km,
Berlin to Warsaw	792 km.

What is the distance shown on each signpost in miles?

2. In some French towns a speed limit of 80 kilometres per hour is imposed. Find this speed limit in miles per hour.

3. Mr and Mrs Blacker on holiday in France are motoring to Nice from Paris. They know the journey is 1 568 km and their car consumes 1 gallon of petrol every 35 miles. Petrol cost one franc per litre.

Find:

a. The distance from Paris to Nice in miles.

b. The number of gallons of petrol needed for the journey.

c. The cost of the petrol in francs.

Miscellaneous questions

1.

Timetable

Distance from London
kilometres

0	London (Euston)	Depart	20.30
133	Rugby	Depart	22.25
255	Crewe	Depart	24.00
294	Warrington	Depart	00.30
313	Wigan	Depart	00.55
338	Preston	Depart	01.15
482	Carlisle	Depart	03.15
672	Stirling	Depart	07.00
725	Perth	Depart	07.45
916	Inverness	Arrive	10.00

From the above timetable answer the following questions:

a. How long did the train take to reach:

Inverness, Stirling, Preston, Wigan, Warrington?

b. How long was the journey between:

Rugby and Wigan, Crewe and Preston, Warrington and Perth?

c. If the train stopped for 6 minutes at Crewe and Preston and 3 minutes at each other station, for how long was the train actually moving?

d. Calculate the average speed of the train between each station. By how much does the fastest speed exceed the average speed for the whole journey?

2. A man takes a holiday in Nice and Florence.

The cost of his hotel at Nice is 29·26 francs each day and he stays there for one week. The hotel in Florence charges 52 500 lire per week.

Calculate in £

a. the cost of a day in the hotel at Nice,

b. the cost of a day in the hotel at Florence,

c. the cost of a fortnight's holiday (in £'s).

d. If an American spent nine days at the hotel in Nice and three weeks in the hotel at Florence, how long would he be able to stay in Germany at an hotel charging 17·76 marks a day, if he had 357 dollars to spend on hotel accommodation?

£1 = 13·3 French francs.

£1 = 1 500 lire.

£1 = 2·38 dollars.

£1 = 9·3 marks.

3. A man wishes to assure his life with an endowment policy for £1000. The annual premiums are £24 for a 'without profits' policy and £36 for a 'with profits' policy. Profits average £3·20 per £100 assured per annum. Both policies qualify for income tax relief at £0·41 in the £ on $\frac{2}{5}$ of the annual premium.

a. How much would he actually pay annually on each policy after allowing for tax relief?

b. Calculate in each case the total sum paid in (less income tax) to the company and the total amount received (including bonuses) at the end of 30 years.

4. A butcher found that it cost £438·90 to run his van during the year 1968–9. This amount included £25·00 car licence, £28·50 insurance and £145·40 for oil, repairs and maintenance. His petrol cost 6p per litre, and he covered 46 200 km in the year.

a. Find how many kilometres he travelled per litre of petrol.

b. What was the overall cost per kilometre?

c. For each £1 spent, what part was spent on:

    i. petrol,

    ii. licence,

    iii. insurance,

    iv. oil, repairs and maintenance?

Express each of these parts as a percentage.

5. A couple decided to purchase a house priced at £3 200. They cannot pay cash down, but a building society is prepared to advance them 85 per cent of the purchase price. The monthly repayments for the loan are at the rate of £0·78 per £100 borrowed for 20 years.

    a. How much will the building society advance? (See note p. 73.)

    b. What cash deposit is required?

    c. How much is the monthly repayment for the loan?

    d. How much would this amount to in 20 years?

    e. What is the total interest paid?

    6. Mrs Brown decides to buy an electric cooker by hire purchase agreement. The cash price of the cooker is £66·25. She agrees to pay a deposit of 10 per cent of the cash price and 12 quarterly instalments of £5·40 each.

    a. Find the deposit.

    b. Calculate the total hire purchase price.

    c. What is the difference between the cash price and the total hire purchase price?

    d. Express the difference as a percentage of the cash price.

    7. Mr Williams earns £2000 per annum. He is married and has two children aged 10 and 14. Mr Evans earns £1850 per annum. He is single. Miss Brown earns £752 per annum.

    Calculate their net weekly income (to the nearest penny), after all deductions have been made, if their superannuation and union contributions* are:

    Mr Williams 4 per cent of salary + £3,

    Mr Evans £5 per annum,

    Miss Brown £5 per annum

and their weekly national insurance contributions are:

    Mr Williams 81p, Mr Evans 94p, Miss Brown 37p.

    8. The following statement shows approximately how the rate in the pound was allocated for a town in 1970–71.

	£
Education	0·50$\frac{1}{2}$
Public Health	0·13$\frac{1}{2}$
Housing	0·03$\frac{1}{2}$
Police and Fire	0·11$\frac{1}{2}$
Highways	0·05$\frac{1}{2}$
Parks and Gardens	0·03
Museum and Library . . .	0·01
Publicity and Planning	0·01$\frac{1}{2}$

£0·90

    * Look at the section on earned income allowance before working this question.

a. Draw a pie chart to represent the information shown on page 122. (Let $0.00\frac{1}{2}p = 2°$.)

b. What percentage of the rates is spent on

(i) Public Health Services?

(ii) Parks and Gardens?

c. The estimated product of a new penny (£0·01) rate is £29 600. What is the total rateable value of the town?

d. If Government grants came to £0·34, thus making the 'Rate in £' payable by Ratepayer = £0·56, what is the total of rates to be collected?

e. What is the estimated expenditure by the Borough in the year 1970–71?

9. Copy out the following table and fill in all the blanks:

Item	Cash price	Deposit	No. of pay-ments	When	How much	Total H.P. price	Difference between H.P. price and cash price
a. High speed cooker	59·75	$5·97\frac{1}{2}$	—	Q	3·95	$69·17\frac{1}{2}$	—
b. Radio	$10·97\frac{1}{2}$	$1·47\frac{1}{2}$	9	M	1·2	—	—
c. Tape recorder	$5·97\frac{1}{2}$	0·60	9	M	0·66	—	—
d. Flying jacket	—	$0·42\frac{1}{2}$	9	M	—	$8·52\frac{1}{2}$	1·05
e. Car radio	$29·97\frac{1}{2}$	4·50	—	M	1·65	34·20	—
f. Amplifier	51·45	$7·82\frac{1}{2}$	12	M	$4·07\frac{1}{2}$	—	—
g. Projector	—	0·30	—	W	0·37	12·14	2·29
h. Food mixer	$7·97\frac{1}{2}$	0·50	32	W	—	9·78	—
j. Guitar	—	2·63	12	M	2·39	—	2·97
k. Zip boots	$4·97\frac{1}{2}$	$0·97\frac{1}{2}$	6	M	—	$5·71\frac{1}{2}$	—
l. Scooter	—	14·50	—	M	2·29	69·46	10·50
m. Watch	$4·47\frac{1}{2}$	$0·27\frac{1}{2}$	32	W	0·17	—	—
n. Dog clippers	8·40	—	8	M	$1·12\frac{1}{2}$	9·25	—
o. Construction kit	—	—	18	F	0·43	9·80	1·40
p. Electric iron	—	—	20	W	0·26	5·20	0·27
q. Washing machine	79·80	None	42	W	2·10	—	—

W = weekly   F = fortnightly   M = monthly   Q = quarterly

Answers

Exercises 1A

1. Andrews £9·02
   Jones £5·98
   Thomas £6·43½
2. No. of hours:

½	4	5	6	7	8	9	10	50
11p	88p	£1·10	£1·32	£1·54	£1·76	£1·98	£2·20	£11

3a. £3·74; b. £5·50; c. £8·47.

4.

	½p	19p	20p	21p	22p	23p	24p	25p
40	20	7·60	8·00	8·40	8·80	9·20	9·60	10·00
40½	20½	7·69½	8·10	8·50½	8·91	9·31½	9·72	10·12½
41	20½	7·79	8·20	8·61	9·02	9·43	9·84	10·25
41½	21	7·88½	8·30	8·71½	9·13	9·54½	9·96	10·37½
42	21	7·98	8·40	8·82	9·24	9·66	10·08	10·50
42½	21½	8·07½	8·50	8·92½	9·35	9·77½	10·20	10·62½
43	21½	8·17	8·60	9·03	9·46	9·89	10·32	10·75
43½	22	8·26½	8·70	9·13½	9·57	10·00½	10·44	10·87½
44	22	8·36	8·80	9·24	9·68	10·12	10·56	11·00
44½	22½	8·45½	8·90	9·34½	9·79	10·23½	10·68	11·12½
45	22½	8·55	9·00	9·45	9·90	10·35	10·80	11·25

5a. £9·60; b. £10·12; c. £9·57; d. £9·22½; e. £10·90½; f. £9·99.

Exercises 1B

a. (i) 20p
   (ii) 27½p
   (iii) 21½p
   (iv) 29p

b. (i) 24p
   (ii) 33p
   (iii) 25½p
   (iv) 34½p

1a.

	Morning	Afternoon	Evening	Total	
Monday	$4\frac{1}{2}$	4	—	$8\frac{1}{2}$	
Tuesday	$4\frac{1}{2}$	$3\frac{1}{2}$	—	8	
Wednesday	$4\frac{1}{4}$	4	—	$8\frac{1}{4}$	
Thursday	$4\frac{1}{2}$	4	$2\frac{1}{2}$	11	
Friday	$4\frac{1}{2}$	4	$2\frac{1}{2}$	11	
					$46\frac{3}{4}$
Saturday	4	3	—	7	
Sunday	—	4	—	4	
					$57\frac{3}{4}$

a.

b.

	Hours	Rate	£
Ordinary Time	42	32p =	13·44
Overtime ($\times 1\frac{1}{4}$)	$4\frac{3}{4}$	40p =	1·90
Overtime ($\times 1\frac{1}{2}$)	7	48p =	3·36
Overtime ($\times 2$)	4	64p =	2·56
	$57\frac{3}{4}$		£21·26

b.

2a. 30p.
 b. 14 hours.
 c. $14 \times 30p = £4\cdot20$.
 d. $42 \times 24p + £4\cdot20 = £14\cdot28$.

	a.	b.	c. (i)	c. (ii)	d. £	e. £
			p	p		
3. Allenbury	42	0	$26\frac{1}{2}$	$31\frac{1}{2}$		8·82
Black	$49\frac{1}{2}$	$5\frac{1}{2}$	$22\frac{1}{2}$	27	1·42	9·34
Crosby	35	0	$27\frac{1}{2}$	33		7·70
Ewart	44	0	35	42		12·32
Foster	$47\frac{1}{2}$	$3\frac{1}{2}$	29	$34\frac{1}{2}$	1·21	11·33
Godden	37	0	$24\frac{1}{2}$	$29\frac{1}{2}$		$7\cdot21\frac{1}{2}$
Hunt	47	3	31	37	0·93	11·71

Note. All fractions have been rounded upwards to the nearest $\frac{1}{2}$p.

4.

	Mon	Tue	Wed	Thur	Fri	Total	Sat	Total
Allen	$8\frac{1}{2}$	$8\frac{1}{2}$	10	$8\frac{1}{2}$	9	$44\frac{1}{2}$	5	$49\frac{1}{2}$
Brown	$9\frac{1}{2}$	10	$5\frac{1}{2}$	12	$12\frac{1}{2}$	$49\frac{1}{2}$	$5\frac{1}{2}$	55
Cook	8	8	9	$7\frac{1}{2}$	3	$35\frac{1}{2}$	0	$35\frac{1}{2}$
Dodds	10	10	8	10	12	50	6	56

$$
\begin{array}{llll}
\text{Brown} & 41 & \text{at } 21\text{ p} & = & 8\cdot61 \\
& 8\tfrac{1}{2} & \text{at } 26\tfrac{1}{2}\text{p} & = & 2\cdot25\tfrac{1}{2} \\
& 5\tfrac{1}{2} & \text{at } 31\tfrac{1}{2}\text{p} & = & 1\cdot73\tfrac{1}{2} \\
\end{array}
$$

£12·60

Cook $35\tfrac{1}{2}$ at 17p   =   £6·03$\tfrac{1}{2}$

$$
\begin{array}{llll}
\text{Dodds} & 43 & \text{at } 24\tfrac{1}{2}\text{p} & = & 10\cdot53\tfrac{1}{2} \\
& 7 & \text{at } 31\text{p} & = & 2\cdot17 \\
& 6 & \text{at } 37\text{p} & = & 2\cdot22 \\
\end{array}
$$

£14·92$\tfrac{1}{2}$

Exercises 1D

1. Hughes £3·80; Roberts £3·50; Thomson £3·00; Williams £3·64.

2. 228; 10 minutes; 316.

3a. £16·27$\tfrac{1}{2}$; *b.* £16·39; *c.* £15·74. ∴ *b.* is the greatest; it exceeds *a.* by 11$\tfrac{1}{2}$p and *c.* by 65p.

4a. (*i*) £10·48, (*ii*) 24p, (*iii*) 4095, (*iv*) £1·42$\tfrac{1}{2}$, (*v*) £12·14$\tfrac{1}{2}$.

  b. (*i*) £2·40, (*ii*) £15·88.

Exercises 1E

1. Week 1 £11·25; Week 2 £17; Week 3 £10; Week 4 £12·50.

2a. (*i*) £4, (*ii*) £11, (*iii*) £7·60.

  b. (*i*) £225, (*ii*) £435.

3. Haberdashery £11·57; Carpets £13·45; Linens £10·10; Bedding £11·00.

4. £30 000.

5. 1966 £2 850; 1967 £3 150; 1968 £3 325; 1969 £3 437·50.

Exercises 1F

1a. £40; *b.* £53·75; *c.* £61·50; *d.* £85·72$\tfrac{1}{2}$.

2a. £560, £610; *b.* £45, £53·33, £58·33; *c.* £21·67.

3a.

	Salary scale A	*Salary scale B*
	£	£
1st year	700	700
2nd year	770	780
3rd year	847	860
4th year	932	940
5th year	1025	1025
6th year	1128	1110
7th year	1241	1195
8th year	1365	1280

b. In the 5th year;
e. During the 7th year;
f. In the 6th year.

Exercises 2A

1a. Mr Styles £936; Miss Brown £702; the Johnson family £1 755.
  b. (*i*) £1 010, (*ii*) £533, (*iii*) £481, (*iv*) £1 145, (*v*) £455.
  c. Mr Foster £295; Mr Styles £403; Miss Brown £221; Mr Johnson £25;
    Mrs Johnson £130.
  d. Mr Foster £114·31; Mr Styles £156·16; Miss Brown £85·64;
    Mr Johnson £9·69; Mrs Johnson £50·38.
2a. £344; *b.* £669; *c.* £879; *d.* £340·61; *e.* £ $\left(\dfrac{1551 - 340·61}{12}\right)$ = £100·86$\frac{1}{2}$.

Exercises 2C

	£	£	50p	10p	5p	2p	1p
1. Bell	19·79	19	1	2	1	2	
Cook	17·09	17			1	2	
Dyson	5·67	5	1	1	1	1	
Evans	5·89	5	1	3	1	2	
Hall	17·61	17	1	1			1
	66·05	63	4	7	4	7	1

$$
\begin{array}{rl}
 & £ \\
63 \times £1 = & 63·00 \\
4 \times 50p = & 2·00 \\
7 \times 10p = & 0·70 \\
4 \times 5p = & 0·20 \\
7 \times 2p = & 0·14 \\
1 \times 1p = & 0·01 \\
\hline
 & £66·05 \\
\end{array}
$$

Exercises 3A

1. £133·76.
2. £73·82.

Exercises 3B

1. £136·14.
2. £31·86.
3a. £199·51; *b.* £127·80; *c.* £273·30.
4. London or Lancashire or Leicestershire County Council, etc.
5. Salary.
6. Standing order and bank charges.

Exercises 3C

1. Credit balance of £132·81 (at end of year).
3. Debit: £63; £13·63.
   Credit: £114; £47·50; £16.
4. £123·87.

Exercises 3D

1.

	Deposit	Withdrawal	Date		Balance
	£	£			£
			March	30th	105·30
	19·50		April	1st	124·80
	25·80			4th	150·60
		50·00		5th	100·60
	19·42			10th	120·02
	15·33			11th	135·35
		30·00		12th	105·35
SO		14·25		12th	91·10
	33·48			17th	124·58
IN	3·21			18th	127·79
		20·00		19th	107·79
	45·00			24th	152·79
		30·00		26th	122·79

Exercises 3E

1.

Date		£
1970		
Oct 23	Balance	425·00
26	Deposit	73·00
		498·00
28	Withdrawal	156·20
		341·80
Nov 5	Deposit	41·27
		383·07
15	Deposit	18·90
		401·97
19	Withdrawal	121·10
		280·87
20	Interest	12·30

		293·17
21	Withdrawal	50·62
		—————
		242·55
Dec 4	Deposit	5·63
		—————
		248·18

Exercises 4C

1. Connexion charge not more than £10; £5 per quarter.
2. £1 per quarter.
    a. Exclusive £6 per quarter
        Shared   £5 per quarter
    b. Exclusive £5 per quarter
        Shared   £4 per quarter.
4. a. 1p *b.* 1p *c.* 2p *d.* 2p *e.* 6p *f.* 3p *g.* 5p
    h. 3p *j.* $37\frac{1}{2}$p *k.* 4p *l.* 18p *m.* 10p *n.* 30p *o.* 9p
    p. $22\frac{1}{2}$p *q.* 45p* *r.* 30p* *s.* 6p *t.* 18p *u.* 34p *v.* 15p
    w. 15p
5. a. 4p *b.* 4p *c.* 8p *d.* 6p *e.* 10p *f.* 4p *g.* 8p
    h. 4p *j.* 40p *k.* 6p *l.* 32p *m.* 20p *n.* 48p *o.* 12p
    p. 26p *q.* 52p* *r.* 52p* *s.* 12p *t.* 30p *u.* 52p *v.* 20p
    w. 24p
6. a. $1\frac{1}{2}$p *b.* $1\frac{1}{2}$p *c.* $1\frac{1}{2}$p *d.* $1\frac{1}{2}$p *e.* 8p *f.* 3p *g.* 9p
    h. 6p *j.* $42\frac{1}{2}$p *k.* 4p (*l* to *w*) as question 4 (*l* to *w*)

Exercises 4E

1a. $7\frac{1}{2}$p; *b.* $12\frac{1}{2}$p; *c.* $17\frac{1}{2}$p; *d.* 75p.

Exercises 4F

1a. yes; *b.* yes; *c.* no; *d.* yes; *e.* yes; *f.* yes; *g.* no; *h.* no; *j.* no.
2a. yes; *b.* yes; *c.* yes; *d.* no; *e.* no; *f.* yes; *g.* no; *h.* yes.
3. £1.
4. £3·$62\frac{1}{2}$.
5a. 15p; *b.* £2·67.
6a. £17·76; £22·49; £20·04; £18·04.
  b. 10p.
  c. £24·80.
  d. $12\frac{1}{2}$ + 10 + 15 = $37\frac{1}{2}$p.
  e. £25·$17\frac{1}{2}$.

* Standard rate.

Exercises 4G

1a. £1; *b.* £1·03; *c.* £1·06; *d.* £1·08; *e.* £1·20; *f.* £1·25.
2a. (*i*) £318, (*ii*) £348, (*iii*) £366.
  b. (*i*) £583, (*ii*) £638, (*iii*) £671.
  c. (*i*) £132·50, (*ii*) £145, (*iii*) £152·50.

Exercises 4H

1a. yes; *b.* no; *c.* yes; *d.* yes; *e.* no; *f.* no.
2a. £12·50; *b.* £25·00; *c.* £87·50; *d.* £125 + £10 repayment on maturity.
3. £2550; 15th March 1971; £625.

Exercises 5A

1a. £1·67$\frac{1}{2}$; *b.* £12·45; *c.* £20·25; *d.* £15·50; *e.* £23·75.
2. £600.
4a. 33$\frac{1}{2}$p; £2·49; £4·05; £3·10; £4·75;
  b. £1·34; £9·96; £16·20; £12·40; £19·00.
5a. 50 years; 41 years; 36 years; 56 years; 38 years;
  b. £83·75; £510·45; £729; £868; £902·50;
  c. £67·00; £408·36; £583·20; £694·40; £722.

Exercises 5B

1. £25·65; £6·75.
2. £2 000; *a.* £5·40; *b.* £100.
3.

Age next birthday	Sum assured	Yearly premium	Quarterly premium
	£	£	£
27	1000	<u>53·00</u>	<u>13·90</u>
20	<u>100</u>	5·08	<u>1·32</u>
22	<u>100</u>	<u>5·11</u>	1·34
<u>24</u>	<u>400</u>	20·60	<u>5·44</u>
25	2000	<u>104</u>	27·40
26	<u>800</u>	Not to exceed £42 £42 exactly	11·04
21	2500	127·25	33·25

4. £1·60 per year or £32   altogether
      2p per year or   40p altogether
      6p per year or £1·20 altogether
    40p per year or £8   altogether
  £2·40 per year or £48   altogether
  £1·12 per year or £22·40 altogether
  £1   per year or £20   altogether

Exercises 5C

1.	Leeds	C	£40
2.	Manchester	D	£33
3.	Hereford	A	£19
4.	Central London	E	£40·70
5.	Brighton	B	£42·93
6.	Exeter	A	*a.* £12; *b.* £9·00
7.	Holyhead	A	£22
8.	Cambridge	B	£35·10
9.	Blackpool	C	*a.* £19·76*; *b.* £16·57$\frac{1}{2}$*
10.	Nottingham	C	£23·80
11.	Glasgow	E	*a.* £16·25; *b.* £14·00
12.	Luton	C	£24·80
13.	Aylesbury	C	£26
14.	Llandudno	A	£18·60
15.	Peterborough	C	*a.* £15·97$\frac{1}{2}$; *b.* £13·95
16.	Cambridge	B	£34
17.	Birkenhead	C	*a.* £17; *b.* £14
18.	Stirling	A	*a.* £15·75*; *b.* £11·70*
19.	Ayr	A	£34·20
20.	Colchester	C	*a.* £9·75; *b.* £9·00
21.	Southampton	B	£46
22.	Tenby	A	£43
23.	Cardiff	C	£37
24.	John o' Groats	A	*a.* £16·79; *b.* £13·60

Exercises 5D

1. a. £4·37$\frac{1}{2}$; *b.* £5; *c.* £4·69
2. (*i*) *a.* £5·62$\frac{1}{2}$; *b.* £6·25; *c.* £5·94
   (*ii*) *a.* £16·25; *b.* £17·50; *c.* £16·87$\frac{1}{2}$
3. Third Party   £6
   Third Party, Fire and Theft   £7·50
   Comprehensive   £27
4a. £15·75; *b.* £16·62$\frac{1}{2}$
5.

	Rating district A–E	Third party premium	Third party fire and theft premium	Comprehensive premium	Comprehensive premium with maximum no-claim discount
		£	£	£	£
a.	B	2·50	3·00	7·50	4·50
b.	C	No insurance available for a 396 cm³ machine for a 17-year-old			
c.	C	5·69	6·56	16·62$\frac{1}{2}$	9·97$\frac{1}{2}$
d.	A	4·37$\frac{1}{2}$	5·62$\frac{1}{2}$	16·25	9·75
e.	B	5·75	6·75	25·00	15·00
f.	C	3·12$\frac{1}{2}$	3·75	10·00	6·00
.	D	6·25	7·25	18·50	11·10

* Note value exceeds £400 therefore premium as shown in table is subject to additional £1.

Exercises 5E

1. House £4·50; Furniture £1·60
2a. (i) £3·75; (ii) £5
  b. (i) £1·50; (ii) £2
  c. (i) £7·50; (ii) £10
  d. (i) £75; (ii) £100
3. (i) a. 40p; b. £1·30; c. £2·40
  (ii) a. 12p; b. 39p; c. 72p
4a. £1·50; b. £1·00; c. £6·87½; d. £4·12½; e. 50p + 90p = £1·40.

Exercises 6A

1. £1552.
2a. June 1965; b. £64·11½.
3. £1460.
4. Brown £1176; Walker £3486; Cape £2204; Riley £779; Small £491.
5a. 8 years 8 months; b. (i) 3 months, (ii) £117·55.

Exercises 6B

1. 8 Dover Road   £2564·34.
  16 Walmer Road   £2072·58.
  35 Park Avenue   £4979·75.
  73 Leamington Road   £3161·10.
  17 Crosby Road   £3564·40.
2. 8 Dover Road   £481·84
  16 Walmer Road   £415·08.
  35 Park Avenue   £857·25.
  73 Leamington Road   £621·60.
  17 Crosby Road   £674·40.
3a. 75 per cent; b. £4608·60; c. £187·40.

Exercises 6C

1a. (i) £16·52 per month
  (ii) £12·88 per month
  (iii) £9·80 per month
b. (i) £3·81 per week
  (ii) £2·97 per week
  (iii) £2·26 per week
2. £356·50.
3a. £4250·00; b. £1356·05; c. £406·35; d. (i) £0·92, (ii) £469·20, (iii) £9·02;
  e. 26·5 per cent.
4. £3750, 75 per cent; £44·06, 17·625 per cent.

Exercises 7A

1. £44; £36·19; £22·95; £52; £77·52; £58·90.
2. (A) 55p; (B) 60p; (C) 64p; (D) 52½p; (E) £170 000; (F) £1 250 000;
  (G) £682 000; (H) £3 156 000.

Exercises 7B

1. £58·24.
  a. £25·48; b. £3·64; c. £29·12.

2.

	(i)	(ii)	(iii)	(iv)
	£	£	£	£
	35·84	47·60	70·56	100·80
a.	15·68	20·82½	30·87	44·10
b.	2·24	2·97½	4·41	6·30
c.	17·92	23·80	35·28	50·40

3. £2 586 000; £1 267 140; £77 580.
4. £76.
6. £120.
7. 11p.
8. £54·56; £64·24.

Exercises 7C

2a. £2·60; b. £135·20; c. £0·95; d. £49·40; e. £3·55; f. £184·60.
g. Town Council; h. Gone on holiday;
j. March/April—end of financial year and budget time;
k. Increase in cost of living—increase in wages, building and maintenance costs.

Exercises 8A

1. 7 rolls.
2a. 7; b. 11; c. 10; d. 7; e. 7 rolls.
3a. (i) 33 m², (ii) about 20 m², (iii) 16·25 m²
b. (i) 12 rolls £5·28; (ii) 7 rolls £6·09; (iii) 8 rolls £5·60.

Exercises 8B

1.

	No. of rolls	£	No. of 0·25 m tiles	Cost £	No. of 0·5 m tiles	Cost £
4 m × 3 m	3	1·35	192	3·84	48	3·84
3·5 m × 4·5 m	4	1·24	252	6·30	63	7·56
4 m square	3	1·56	256	7·68	64	10·24
7 m × 3·5 m	5	3·00	392	19·96	98	23·52

2.

	(i)	(ii)	(iii) £
Ex. A. Question 1.	12	3	1·35
Ex. A. Question 2. a.	12	3	1·35
b.	28	6	2·70
c.	24	6	2·70
d.	12	4	1·80
e.	14	3	1·80

2. Continued

		(i)	(ii)	(iii) £
Ex. A. Question 3.	(*i*)	33	6	2·70
	(*ii*)	20	4	1·80
	(*iii*)	16	4	1·80

Exercises 8C

	(*i*)	(*ii*)	(*iii*)
1a.	5·5 m²	½ litre	60p
b.	10 m²	1 litre	£1·05
c.	6·5 m²	½ litre	60p

2.

	Area in m²	Undercoat required litres	Gloss required litres	Undercoat cost £	Gloss cost £	Total £
a.	7	1½	1	1·12	0·92	2·04
b.	12	2	1	1·44	0·92	2·36
c.	15	2½	1½	1·84	1·42	3·26
d.	11	2	1	1·44	0·92	2·36
e.	6	1	½	0·72	0·50	1·22

Exercises 8D

1.

	(*a*)	(*b*) £	(*c*) £
(*i*)	144	12·50	5·78
(*ii*)	64	5·50	2·88
(*iii*)	108	9·25	4·86
(*iv*)	217	18·00	9·76
(*v*)	154	13·25	7·02
(*vi*)	35	3·75	1·66

Exercises 8E

1. £15·64   *2.* £22·08   *3.* £47·84   *4.* £41·86; £5·98.
5a. £4·80; *b.* £14·00; *c.* £3·03; *d.* £4·90; *e.* £2·05; *f.* £7·50; *g.* £5·95; *h.* £3·50.

Exercises 9A

1. 50 000   *2.* 8 000   *3.* 200
4. 90   *5.* 6   *6.* 48 375; 19 018

Exercises 9B

	units
1. Quarter ending 27th April	1 690
Quarter ending 16th July	1 060

1. Continued

	units
Quarter ending 19th October	922
Quarter ending 14th January	2219
Quarter ending 17th April	1852
Quarter ending 25th July	1396

4. 8 to 9 (average 8·8) units.

Exercises 9C

1a. 3 units, 7·2p
b. $\frac{3}{8}$ unit, 0·6p
c. 32 minutes, $1\frac{1}{3}$ unit
d. 2p, 9 units
e. 1 hour 36 min, 2 units
f. $2\frac{1}{2}$p, 4 units
g. $2\frac{1}{2}$ kW, 5 units
h. $2\frac{1}{4}$ kW $2\frac{5}{8}$ units

Exercises 9D

1.

	Tariff A £	Tariff B £
1690	16·61	17·56
1060	10·94	11·26
922	9·70	9·88
2219	21·37	22·85
1852	18·07	19·18
1396	13·96	14·62

2. 740 units; £8·06.

Exercises 9E

1. £28·55; £32·55; £42·15.
3. £20·30; £14 + £4·35 = £18·35.

Exercises 9F

	m^3
1. April 1969	58140
July 1969	58900
Oct 1969	59380
Jan 1970	62100
April 1970	65850
July 1970	67410

2a. 760 m^3; *b.* 480 m^3; *c.* 2720 m^3; *d.* 3750 m^3; *e.* 1560 m^3.
4a. Just prior to October 1969.
b. Approximately 1692 m^3 per quarter.
5a. 3960 m^3.
b. 1320; 740; 560; 1340 m^3.

Exercises 9G

1a. 60p; *b.* £1·11; *c.* £1·56.
2a. 54 m^3; *b.* 105 m^3.

3. (*i*) 100 therms £4·80.
   (*ii*) 254 therms, £11·73.

Exercises 9H

1a. 16 therms £4·35; *b.* 112 therms £22·35; *c.* 192 therms £37·35.

	B	C	D
2a.	£1·35 + £16·20 = £17·55	£3·35 + £14·58 = £17·93	£9·35 + £13·50 = £22·85
b.	1125	1204	1454

3.   B £20·10; C £20·22$\frac{1}{2}$; D £24·97$\frac{1}{2}$
  a. B
  b. B
  c. C or D
4a. (*i*) No answer; (*ii*) 667 m^3; (*iii*) 1 600 m^3; (*iv*) 3 000 m^3;
  b. (*i*)   —   (*ii*) £21·35; (*iii*) £49·35;   (*iv*) 84·35;
  c. Tariff A.
  d. (*i*) 667 m^3; (*ii*) D rather than B at 1 600 m^3
                    D rather than C at 3 000 m^3.

Exercises 10B

1a. 37$\frac{1}{2}$p £7·12$\frac{1}{2}$; *b.* 11p £4·29; *c.* − £6·45; *d.* 18$\frac{1}{2}$p £7·21$\frac{1}{2}$.
2a. £47·88; *b.* £22·46; *c.* £28·08; *d.* £3·46; *e.* £37·62.

Exercises 10C

1. £585; £526·50; £473·85.
2. £200; £160; £128.
3. £84; £58·80; £41·16.
4. £75·60; £68·04; £61·24.
5. £2 975; £2 528·75; £2 149·44.
6. £4 375; £3 828·12$\frac{1}{2}$; £3 349·61.

Exercises 10D

1a. £119·50; *b.* £59·95; *c.* £102·90.
2a. £11·95 + £126·72; *b.* £9 + £59·40; *c.* £15·65 + £97·80.
3a. £138·67; *b.* £68·40; *c.* £113·45.
4a. £19·17; *b.* £8·45; *c.* £10·55.

5a. $\dfrac{1917}{11950}$; 16 per cent; *b.* $\dfrac{169}{1199}$; 14·1 per cent; *c.* $\dfrac{211}{2058}$; 10·25 per cent.

Exercises 10E

1. £10·68; 17·8 per cent or 8·9 per cent per annum.
2. £7·12; 24·2 per cent per annum.
3. £81·32$\frac{1}{2}$; 19·2 per cent or 4·8 per cent per annum.
4. £67·48; 19 per cent or 4·75 per cent per annum.
5. £0·92; 13·2 per cent or 17·6 per cent per annum.

Exercises 10F

1. £3·07;   4·2 per cent per annum
2. £2·31.
3. £33·74;   £29·93.
4. £3·32.

Exercises 11A

1a. 07.50; *b.* 24.00; *c.* 18.30; *d.* 12.00; *e.* 00.05; *f.* 23.55; *g.* 21.45.
2a. 7.40 a.m.; *b.* 7.36 p.m.; *c.* half an hour past midnight; *d.* 3.45 p.m.; *e.* 7.20 p.m.;
  f. 9.50 p.m.; *g.* 1.10 p.m.
3a. 0.15; *b.* 54 km/h; *c.* (*i*) 23.45, 00.15; (*ii*) 63 km/h.
4. 72 km/h.

Exercises 11B

		Train A	Train B
1a.	(*i*)	10 minutes	11 minutes
	(*ii*)	2 hours 20 minutes	2 hours 15 minutes
	(*iii*)	2 hours 43 minutes	2 hours 39 minutes
	(*iv*)	5 hours 55 minutes	6 hours 12 minutes
	(*v*)	3 hours 12 minutes	3 hours 33 minutes
	(*vi*)	6 hours 47 minutes	7 hours 10 minutes
	(*vii*)	52 minutes	58 minutes

  b. 1 hour 30–33 minutes approximately.
  c. Saturday. Cross-country through trains like these only run to convey passengers to and from seaside resorts at the beginning and end of their holiday.
2a. Yes.
  b.

	Train A	Train B
(*i*)	49·5 km/h	50·5 km/h
(*ii*)	69 km/h	62 km/h
(*iii*)	54 km/h	48·5 km/h
(*iv*)	59 km/h	56·5 km/h

  c. 1·2p.
  d. Crewe (train B) or Wolverhampton (both trains).
3a. 128 km; *b.* 174 km; *c.* 61 km; *d.* 79 km; *e.* 39 km; *f.* 64 km.
4a. 14.30; *b.* 16.35; *c.* 17.40; *d.* 22.28.

	h	*min*		*h*	*min*		*h*	*min*
5a.	1	56	*b.* 1	1		*c.* 3		
	1	33			43		2	18
	1	44			47		2	32
	1	41			55		2	37
	2	5		1	5		3	12
	1	44			49		2	35
	2	7			58		3	10
	1	52			58		2	51

6. 58 km/h; 76 km/h; 69 km/h; 67 km/h; 54·5 km/h; 67·5 km/h; 55 km/h; 61 km/h.
8a. 14.30; *b.* 19.30; *c.* 12.30; *d.* 11.30; *e.* 15.35; *f.* 14.30.

Exercises 11C

1.

	a. (francs)	b. (lire)	c. (dollars)
(i)	332·5	37 500	59·5
(ii)	1 602·65	180 750	286·79
(iii)	111·39	12 562½	19·93
(iv)	260·97	29 430	46·70
(v)	94·96	10 710	16·99
(vi)	51·47	5 805	9·21

2a. £9·25; b. £20; c. £5·20; d. £6·60; e. £116·28.

Exercises 11D

1. $67\frac{1}{2}$ miles; 340 miles; 480 miles; 495 miles.
2. 50 mile/h.
3a. 980 miles; b. 28 gallons; c. 128 francs.

Miscellaneous questions

1a. $13\frac{1}{2}$ hours; $10\frac{1}{2}$ hours; $4\frac{3}{4}$ hours; 4 hours 25 minutes; 4 hours.
 b. $2\frac{1}{2}$ hours; $1\frac{1}{4}$ hours; $7\frac{1}{4}$ hours.
 c. 13 hours.
 d. Speeds in km/h: 71·5; 79·5; 86; 35·2; 85; 74·5; 51·5; 76; 86·5.
    Average speed for journey 70·5; Fastest speed is 16 km/h faster.
2a. £2·20; b. £5·00; c. £50·40; d. 14 days.
3a. £20·06; £30·10.
 b. £601·80; £903; £1000; £1960.
4a. 11·55 km per gallon; b. 0·95p; c. (i) 54·7%, (ii) 5·7%, (iii) 6·5%, (iv) 33·1%.
5a. £2 700; b. £500; c. £21·06; d. £5 054·40; e. £2 354·40.
6a. £6.62½; b. £71·42½; c. £5·17½; d. 7·8 per cent.
7. Mr Williams £30·38 based on £1 920 net; Mr Evans £26·33;
   Miss Brown £12·08.
8b. (i) 15 per cent; (ii) $3\frac{1}{3}$ per cent
 c. £2 960 000
 d. £1 657 600
 e. £2 664 000

9a. 16   £9·42½   b. £12·27½   £1·30   c. £6·54   £0·56½
 d. £7·47½   £0·90   e. 18   £4·22½   f. £56·72½ £5·27½
 g. £9·85   32   h. £0·29   £1·80½   j. £28·34   £31·31
 k. £0·79   £0·74   l. £58·96   24   m. £5·71½   £1·24
 n. £0·25   £0·85   o. £8·40   £2·06   p. £4·93   none
             q. £88·20   £8·40.